Pa
to
A Wilderness
Honeymoon

Cliff Kopas

TouchWood Editions Ltd.
Victoria, BC, Canada
This book is distributed by The Heritage Group, #108–17665 66A Avenue, Surrey,
BC, Canada, V3S 2A7.

Cover: Background photo by Nicholas Newbeck Design; inset by Cliff and Ruth
Kopas. Maps: Adapted from the originals by John Callan. Cover and book design:
Nancy St.Gelais. Editor: Karla Decker.
This book is set in Goudy.

TouchWood Editions acknowledges the financial support for its publishing program
from The Canada Council for the Arts, the Government of Canada through the
Book Publishing Industry Development Program (BPIDP) and the Province of
British Columbia through the British Columbia Arts Council.

Printed and bound in Canada by Friesens, Altona, Manitoba.

National Library of Canada Cataloguing in Publication Data

Kopas, Cliff, 1911-1978
    Packhorses to the Pacific : a wilderness honeymoon /Cliff Kopas. – 1st
TouchWood ed.

Includes index.

ISBN 1-894898-13-3

    1. Kopas, Cliff, 1911-1978. 2. Packhorse camping—British Columbia.
3. Packhorse camping—Rocky Mountains, Canadian (B.C. and Alta.)
4. British Columbia—Description and travel. 5. Rocky Mountains, Canadian
(B.C. and Alta.)—Description and travel. I. Title.

FC3817.3.K66 2004   917.1104'3   C2004-900402-6

BRITISH
COLUMBIA
ARTS COUNCIL
We acknowledge the support of the Province of British Columbia
through the British Columbia Arts Council

The Canada Council | Le Conseil des Arts
for the Arts | du Canada

DEDICATED TO THE MEMORY OF RUTH,
WHOSE NAME ALSO SPELLED COURAGE

CONTENTS

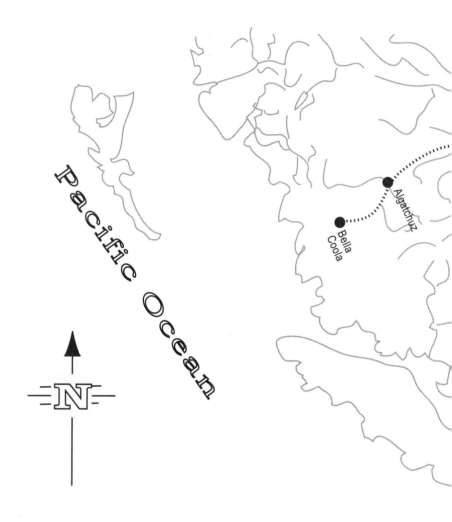

Pacific Ocean

N

Algatchuz

Bella
Coola

The Journey ⋅......'''''''''....
Border ▬■━⋅■━⋅■━

FOREWORD

On the morning of June 17, 1933, Cliff and Ruth Kopas got married. In the afternoon, they set off on a four-month, 1,500-mile journey from Okotoks, Alberta, to Bella Coola, B.C. To guide and help them, the 22-year-old horse lover and his 23-year-old bride, who had never ridden a horse, had only Cliff's childhood dream of following Alexander Mackenzie's path to the Pacific, their five packhorses and, most importantly, their mutual love and dedication.

Sixty-eight years later, on July 1, 2001, my wife Joanne and I left Calgary for a three-day drive to Bella Coola. Our purpose was to dedicate a new headstone to my mother, Ruth, who was Cliff's companion, his first true love and biggest supporter. My family has grown up with the story of *Packhorses* and my father's other stories, lovingly related to them by my sister, Rene Morton, my father's legend teller.

As we sped along the paved highways of Alberta and British Columbia, we pondered the words of *Packhorses* and tried to imagine the experience of this young couple as they slogged over snow-covered mountain passes, through dense forest and across raging rivers. Our evenings were spent in the comfort of motels with clean, dry sheets and maid service, a far cry from the do-it-yourself cooking and camp-making that Cliff and Ruth would have faced day after day, often in bad weather. As we descended

Their mission to follow in Alexander Mackenzie's footsteps to the Pacific accomplished, Ruth and Cliff Kopas stand on a cairn commemorating the great explorer's journey.

"the Hill" into the luxuriant valley of the Bella Coola River, we felt overwhelmed by the magnitude of my parents' journey and a sense of the emotional and physical hardships they had endured in order to live their dream. The dedication of the headstone took on a new meaning for me; their story was indeed a legacy to be passed on to our grandchildren, a story of love and accomplishment that we are proud to share.

Join me as we journey back to 1933, when these two young lovers embarked on their first shared journey with only a couple of dollars in their pockets and the best wishes of their friends and parents.

Except for the difficult (but passable) Goat River Trail portion, from McBride to Bowron Lake, most of the trail taken by Alexander Mackenzie and later by my parents can be viewed today from the comfort of one's car. If you are blessed with an adventurous spirit, I invite you to hike the Goat River Trail and then finish your journey by car with the breathtaking descent into the Bella Coola Valley. If you prefer armchair travel by a cozy fireplace, sit back with this new edition of *Packhorses to the Pacific* and relive Cliff and Ruth's adventure. It is a story of challenges overcome by steadfast love, determination and companionship, a story that proves you can conquer impossible odds if you have the fortitude to believe in your dreams. Enjoy my parents' story!

Keith Cole

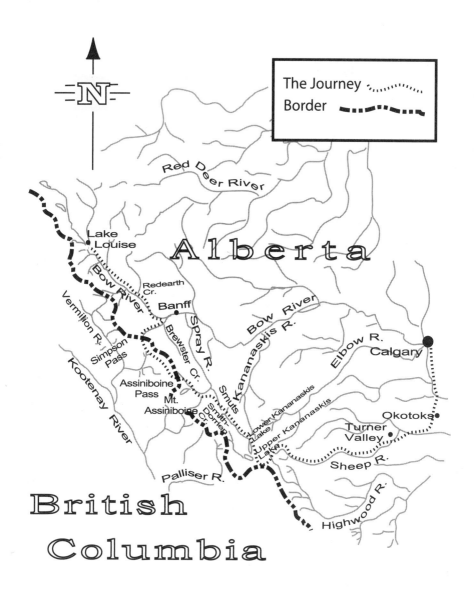

The Journey ⋯⋯⋯⋯

Border ▄▬▄▬▄▬

Red Deer River

Alberta

Lake Louise

Bow River

Redearth Cr.

Banff

Spray R.

Bow River

Brewster Cr.

Kananaskis R.

Elbow R.

Calgary

Vermillion R.

Simpson Pass

Assiniboine Pass

Mt. Assiniboine

Smuts

Smith Dorrien

Lower Kananaskis Lake

Upper Kananaskis Lake

Okotoks

Turner Valley

Kootenay River

Palliser R.

Sheep R.

British Columbia

Highwood R.

ADVENTURE BECKONS

Three hours after our wedding in Calgary, Ruth and I set out on a journey through the wilderness to the Pacific Coast. All we possessed in the world was our clothes, minimal camping equipment, five horses and $2.65 in cash.

Not everyone's idea of a honeymoon, perhaps, but the year was 1933, and by the standards of those desperate days we were lucky. Almost rich.

I had dreamed of doing such a trip ever since an enthusiastic schoolteacher had talked of the early history of western Canada, which, though brief, is crammed with dramatic stories of explorers, pioneers, fur traders, gold seekers, railway men and every kind of adventurer. With my friend Neil MacKay, and gear and horses supplied by our parents, I had spent several summer holidays in the mountains, where we had both learned valuable lessons of a kind not taught in school.

But now I was older and wanted to go on a much longer expedition, and Neil could not be spared from the family business. True, I had other friends who would have been glad to come along, but they were either unsuitable or had no money, for soon after we all left school, the stock market crashed, and by now Canada was in the grip of the Depression.

Without the right companion, the trip would be doomed before we left home, and I was about to abandon the whole scheme when my

1

fiancée, Ruth Hall, offered to come with me. This was a wonderful idea, and we immediately began making preparations to cover everything from maps to ministers, bridal clothes to saddle packs.

Our plan was to follow the trail of Alexander Mackenzie near Quesnel to the Pacific at Bella Coola. Mackenzie reached the site of present-day Quesnel by canoe. We would travel by horses, starting into the wilderness west of Okotoks, on Sheep Creek, to reach the Kananaskis Lakes through Elbow Pass. We would then angle northwest along the spine of the continent, across the wildest part of British Columbia to reach salt water at Bella Coola, just under the 53rd parallel of north latitude. I estimated the trip would take four months.

So on that June day after the service and a brief reception, we set out. Ahead of us were 1,500 trail miles, three mountain ranges and some of the roughest terrain in North America. But what of it? We were young, eager for adventure and without a care in the world. It didn't even worry us that Ruth had never ridden before and knew nothing about horses.

She soon began to learn. The first job when we made camp was to supervise our five while they grazed, and then secure them to prevent escape; we had no wish to go back to the prairies in search of runaways. Four were haltered, but the gentle O'Hara (so named because I had bought him at Lake O'Hara) became frantic if tied by the head, yet a mere string attached to his fetlock was sufficient to hold him.

The second day we weren't so lucky. They hadn't got away in the night, but when we put them out with hobbles and drags while we made breakfast, they decided they were not hungry but homesick. They didn't want to leave the prairies, they didn't like the mountains, and they definitely didn't fancy going all the way to the ocean.

We found our two saddle mounts not far down the road, but the three pack animals had pulled their drags over five miles and would have gone farther had not the caretaker at Indian Oils, the wildcat oil well farthest west of Turner Valley, caught and held them for us.

Back at camp we reassembled packs that seemed as big and awkward as haystacks. O'Hara threw himself when his was almost complete,

While the rest of the world swelters on a blistering hot day in late June, packhorses and people stay cool on top of Sheep Creek Pass, Alberta.

necessitating a repack job, but the red mare gave no trouble, so in the end I led her out of camp at the head of a small procession, with Ruth at the rear to see that none of the others broke rank. Everything went well until we turned west again. Then they seemed to realize this was not the way home, and when Ruth would not let them go east, they dashed back to camp. Their packs were more haystackish than ever and needed tightening, and after we had done this, Ruth led the way while I followed. We managed to cross Bluerock Canyon bridge and get about half a mile through Jack pines and up a short steep climb. Then I saw the bay's pack turn. This was a sure sign of trouble, and I dismounted and shouted to Ruth to stop. At the same moment the bay panicked, reared, tore away from her and, with the speed and weight of a rock slide, crashed down the slope straight toward me. I leaped into a pile of slash below the road.

When I surfaced, the noise was diminishing in the distance, but the only horse in sight was Ruth's, and even that one was straining to rush after the others. Food, dishes, clothes and our tent had been flung to the four winds.

Seizing Ruth's horse and leaving her totally alone, I dashed off in pursuit. Two of the runaways were only a quarter of a mile away, so I took these back to Ruth before galloping eastward again, fearing the other two would once more get as far as Indian Oils, or even farther. It was a great relief when I found them, but they required considerable persuasion to turn west again, and by the time we reached Ruth, she was on the point of coming in search for me.

We decided not to risk any more equine violence, and after retrieving our belongings, we made camp at the first suitable spot. Over the evening meal we took stock of events, noting 12 hours of strenuous activity between meals; 25 miles of travel for some of the horses; battered goods and gear. In addition, Ruth was extensively bruised and my hands were burned by rope; she had been left alone in the wilderness long enough to be frightened, and we had accomplished only three miles of our journey.

The next morning only two horses were missing, the other three having been tied to trees. The missing horses, hobbled, had again tried to return to the prairies, but were soon found and brought back, and packing was accomplished without incident. Some hours later, having made a successful crossing of Sheep Creek where there had once been a bridge, we were at Burns' mine.

The mine, dug into the base of Storm Mountain, was one of the many enterprises of Senator Pat Burns. Frontiersman, cattle king, rancher, timber man, meat packer: Burns was a driving spirit from Calgary. We had crossed one of his ranches west of Turner Valley. The road we had travelled into the mountains had been a Burns endeavour, and here was a mine he had started to develop. A railroad had been planned up the Sheep Creek Valley over the road that our horses had tried so hard to use as an escape route. Coal had been hauled out by the wagonload, cutting deep ruts, but the project had been shelved, perhaps because of the Depression, or perhaps because of all the gas discovered in Turner Valley, whence more than one boom had rippled into Okotoks, Calgary and across the continent.

The first discovery well had produced a short-lived boom in 1914. Then some impatient individuals tried to create another by pouring crude oil into the waters of Sheep Creek just below a well that was being drilled. The well did prove to be a producer; the intended victims made a modest bit of money, and the culprits who had tried to salt the well went to jail, all in good storybook fashion.

When Royalite Four blew in 1924, lifting a column of well casing high into the air, the fire that caught, both at the base and at the tip of the column, created a beacon that could be seen for a hundred miles over the platter-flat prairies. The valley was lit as if by sunlight, and at nighttime, under the right cloud conditions, it looked as if the sun had just set.

Gas was in excess, and flares burning it off varied in size from the roaring inferno of Hell's Half Acre, unapproachable at 200 yards, to small flares perpetually burning to incinerate the garbage of restaurateurs, retailers or housewives. The tantalizing odours of table refuse roasting and boiling in these pits incited pigs to escape from their pens, and when they closed in to collect the goodies, the hair was scorched off their bodies. Similarly, dogs had their heads and forequarters singed bald.

Turner Valley lured more than oil kings, and in the early '30s, hungry, homeless, jobless men discovered they could sleep, winter or summer, in the warmth of the flames, even though they did sometimes have to compete for space with bald dogs and nude pigs.

Flowers bloomed all winter within the circle of warmth, even though beyond the influence of the flames the temperature might be 40 below zero.

Ruth stands outside the tent at the first camp (June 17–19).

Mount Gibraltar beckons in the distance as Ruth and Cliff hit the trail in earnest on June 20.

Miles of pipeline, coated three or four inches thick with ice, lay white on the ground when the expanding gases within them acted as a refrigerant to collect and freeze the water vapour in the air, but an old-timer who had no truck with scientific explanations declared, "Any tarnation damn fool would know you're going to tap into hell if you go drilling holes that far down."

Since those early days, Sheep Creek had converted the wagon road to a pack-trail by washing out the bridge, and the mine had become a favourite stopping place for westbound travellers.

A watchman had been kept on, a big Swiss with a huge mountaineer's pipe and a hospitable heart. But he had died last winter and no one answered our halloos. It seemed a lonely haunted place now, and we pushed on a mile or two and camped among some scattered Christmas trees.

This was a good campsite with the last grass until Kananaskis Lakes, a long day's journey westward. Here Sheep Creek burbled through an open park where last winter's snows still glowed like white linen among the trees. Here a ring of peaks, all 10,000 feet

The campsite at Lower Kananaskis Lake is a springboard to high adventure in the mountains.

7

Ruth prepares a meal inside the tent.

or more, reached skyward: Gibraltar to the east, coal-stuffed Storm Mountain behind us, and Cougar and Burns mountains to the north. When purple dusk spread from the shadows, it seemed our campfire was a big star lent to us for the evening.

To assure that our horses stayed to appreciate it after grazing, we tied all of them to trees.

But horse trouble hit us hard the next morning when the red mare decided against being a beast of burden. When we were about to fasten her pack down with the diamond hitch, she exploded into violence, broke her halter rope and scattered her pack, as she had done two days earlier. We replaced the broken rope and tried again to pack her. This time she threw the boxes even sooner. We rigged a lariat to her feet so she couldn't buck, whereat she threw herself on the ground. When we let her up and tried again, she repeated the process and broke more rigging.

We finally admitted she was too much for us. Besides the precious ropes she had broken, we were poorer by the fact that one tin of powdered milk and another of syrup had sprung open in one of the boxes, creating a mess that would be with us for a long time. The little change purse carrying our total treasury of $2.65 was recovered, now less a silver dollar and a souvenir five-cent piece that must have been flung farther than the others. Our combined capital was now $1.60.

We couldn't afford to fight the horse. What could we do with her? Ominously, with the knowledge of many an historical mountain trip that had sacrificed horses to stave off starvation, we called her Hash.

The other mare, a tawny buckskin, accepted the pack without a tremble. We called her Dream.

We had hoped to start at 10 o'clock, but it was noon before we began climbing over the summit of Sheep Creek on wind-packed snow. Then we dropped down into the upper end of Elbow Valley to wallow for a distressing half-hour through stirrup-deep snow around Elbow Lake, which lay white and frozen at the top of the pass. Easing into the Pocaterra Creek defile, we discovered fresh horse tracks on the trail, which encouraged us with the thought that winter windfall across the trail would be chopped clear, and coasted down the long easy grade to Lower Kananaskis Lake.

Within talking distance of the Lady of the Lake we built a roaring fire at 7:30 in the evening to shake off the chill of the clouds that had swept down and spat at us.

The Lady of the Lake was a four-foot-tall carving of an Indian maiden, presiding in mute and nude dignity over the campsite where a big spring of ice-cold water bubbled out of the forest floor. In 1926 (the date was carved in the tree beneath the little statue) Jack Fuller, a red-haired packer with a group of fishermen from the eastern States, had found time, an axe and a hunting knife on his hands, and combining these with his artistic talent one afternoon, he had created the Lady. Comely she was and obviously sweet-tempered, reflecting that the trip Fuller was currently on was a good one. Had it not been, Jack might have

Ruth sits contentedly atop Dream, a tawny buckskin who accepted her pack without a tremble.

10

carved, as he had done elsewhere, an ill-tempered harridan with horseshoes driven into it. He had spent a portion of his boyhood among the prairie Indians. They liked each other; the squaws laughed with delight as they ran their fingers through his luxuriant red locks, and he created their likenesses in wood.

Besides Fuller's friend, there was a table and benches built by someone for kitchen convenience, and someone else had built a good stout pole fence to keep horses from wandering.

It was a good camp.

It was also a hub from which trails radiated like spokes on a wheel: the Pocaterra Creek trail to the east, the twin passes to the Elk River to the south, the high and haunting Kananaskis Passes to the west, the Mud Lake Pass to the northwest, leading to Spray Lakes and Banff or to Mount Assiniboine and finally the main trail down the Kananaskis River to the railway and Canmore. No matter which way one looked, it was the springboard to high adventure in the mountains.

The Lady of the Lake, carved by packer Jack Fuller in 1926, presides in mute, nude dignity over a campsite at Kananaskis Lake.

11

It had almost been the jumping-off place to eternity some 80 years previously for a party of 100 men, women and children, some of them suckling infants, who became lost, starved and snowbound until they finally escaped through three feet of snow over the barren pass leading to the Palliser River and the Pacific Coast.

The leader of the group, James Sinclair, was an extraordinary man, the son of a half-breed mother and a Hudson's Bay Company factor, a man with a Cambridge University education and thorough knowledge of life in the Canadian wilds. Sometimes working for the company, and sometimes as a free trader working against it, he was in 1854 the company's choice to lead a party of settlers to the Oregon coast. Anticipating a dispute between Britain and the United States over ownership of the Oregon territory, the Hudson's Bay Company was virtually sponsoring the emigration of Canadians to the west coast to bolster British claims there. Sinclair had made up his mind that he wished to live in the far west, so quickly arranged to lead the party.

He had been leader of a similar expedition 13 years before and thought he knew what to expect.

The party, which set out in 1854 from Fort Garry (now Winnipeg) with Red River carts and 250 head of oxen, included 11 married women, some unmarried girls and many children and several infants. Sinclair's wife, his infant son and a delicate 19-year-old daughter were among the travellers.

The day of their departure from Fort Garry was marked by a total eclipse of the sun, bringing midnight darkness in the middle of the day, a terrified halt to all activities and, to the superstitious, premonitions of evil.

Progress across the plains, slow enough because of the oxen, was at first impeded by the presence of 300 sheep that settler Sutherland insisted on taking with him. This impediment was removed in a night of horror and carnage at Fort Pitt when two or three hundred sleigh dogs, summer-idle and semi-starved and almost as savage as the wolves that in most part constituted their ancestry, broke forth from their enclosures. In a barking, baying bloodbath that lasted the whole of a summer's night they killed all the sheep.

At the height of this ghastly holocaust a baby was born to one of the women of Sinclair's party.

When they were leaving Fort Pitt, Sinclair was intercepted by a party of Cree Indians under Chief Mackipictoon, who, 13 years before, had guided him with an even bigger party through the mountains via White Man Pass. Now the Cree party accompanied the Sinclair party to Fort Edmonton, each affording the other protection from marauding Blackfoot.

At the same time Mackipictoon endeavoured to sell Sinclair the idea of hiring him as a guide. He assured Sinclair that there was a route along which carts could be taken all the way. The chief, who was also called Broken Arm, had in 1840 been Missionary Rundle's first convert to Christianity. Had he not previously successfully guided Sinclair through the high mountains? Now he knew a better route, one good enough for wheels. Sinclair, not entirely convinced that the Cree chief had accepted Christian honesty along with the new faith, hired him as guide, but at Fort Edmonton had his own men trained in the art of packing and throwing the diamond hitch.

Always with a wary eye for any sign of the Blackfoot, the party left Fort Edmonton, and, angling toward the mountains, entered them by way of the Bow Valley and came to Strong Current River, the Kananaskis. Here, with mounting doubts about his guide, Sinclair camped for two weeks while he and his men, using hand-forged nails and wood from their Red River carts, made packsaddles and trained their oxen to be pack animals.

At this camp, too, another baby was born, but it survived only a few days.

The wild, canyon-cut country of the Kananaskis treated the party cruelly. There was no trail, and they fought fallen timber, bridged chasms and suffered in mountain torrents. Above them rose titanic peaks from which hanging glaciers dropped cannonading cascades of ice. There was little grass for the stock, and game was so scarce that some of their cattle had to be butchered for food. Finally, to a camp gripped in despair, the guide admitted he was hopelessly lost, that he had never been this way before. Surviving one disaster after another, they eventually escaped, presumably over South Kananaskis Pass, 7,439 feet high, dropping to the Palliser, Kootenay and Columbia rivers.

The previous trip Sinclair had made with the same guide through the 7,112-foot White Man Pass had taken 10 days. This one took 30 days, and Sinclair said it was the roughest trail he had ever followed.

Four years later, in August of 1858, Captain Palliser, intrigued by Sinclair's reports, set out personally to investigate the Kananaskis route with hopes that it might be suitable for a railway. So drastically did his findings disagree with Sinclair that some historians wonder if he did actually follow the same route or if instead he took one of the easier, more obvious Elk Passes. A trail created by the passage of 250 head of cattle, some requiring a wider path because of their packs, could not have been obliterated in four years, yet Palliser could find no trace of it.

Historians are also puzzled by Palliser's reports. He intimated that the approach to Kananaskis Pass was surprisingly easy and it is generally supposed he used the higher, more northerly of the twin passes. His data does not bear minute comparison with today's findings. The approach to the south pass, 7,439 feet, is a clawing, back-humping scramble up scree slopes; and to the north pass, 7,682 feet, is in part up a steep slope thickly covered with spruce growth swept and mowed and stunted by snow-slides and as tough and unfriendly as barbed wire. The actual summit is small rubble, snow-covered most of the year and offering no place, contrary to his suggestion, to camp where you could dip a kettle into either the Pacific watershed or the Saskatchewan River system.

We awoke next morning to a sparkling day and Ruth decided a washday was necessary. Washing clothes on the trail? Never done! Then we'll institute something new ... and we did. When the clothes were washed and neatly hung on a length of rope, we took our saddle horses and splashed across the broad shallow ford of the river connecting the two lakes, and on sunny prominences above Upper Kananaskis Lake we basked in the sunshine, listened to the distant pulsating roar of Panther Falls and admired the peaks and glaciers surrounding them.

We returned to camp just in time to rescue our laundry, not from a suddenly modest Lady of the Lake but from a young deer who intended to eat it, and to see a big black squirrel pack off a bar of soap that we had left on the table beside the wash basin. The deer bounded away when Ruth shouted, but the squirrel barked indignantly, frothing at the mouth from soap.

The forest ranger, "Mack" Mackenzie, an acquaintance of three summers, found us and invited us to his cabin for supper. He had come out from Canmore a week ago. It was his horses' tracks we had come on just below the snows of Elbow Pass. He had seen the snow and was surprised we had got through. He had heard all the high passes were snow-plugged.

"Where are you going from here?" he asked.

We told him we were aiming at Mount Assiniboine by way of Smith-Dorrien Creek, Mud Lake Pass and the Spray River.

"Smith-Dorrien is in spring spate," he declared. "Stay here for a couple of days and let it run off. Be my guests."

Had we stayed, the way he fed us would have forced him into an early trip to Canmore for more food. But we had a date at Lake Louise for July 1, Ruth's birthday, and already we were behind schedule.

Early next afternoon we faced the first crossing of Smith-Dorrien. We dropped easily down the seven-mile length of Lower Kananaskis Lake, crossed its outlet on a comfortable bridge and started westering up Smith-Dorrien. Now, high and horrifying, its savage muttering verified Mackenzie's statement that it was at the height of its annual free-for-all, devil-take-the-intruder rampage.

Fording the stream here was a nasty experience. A bridge had once spanned the creek, but its gaunt remains high up in the trees showed what the stream had thought of that arrangement.

We decided we would postpone the crossing until next morning when, after a cold night, melting would be at a minimum and the stream level the lowest. A good campsite close by invited and we accepted. The night was the warmest of the trip, the mosquitoes never retired and the stream called its endless challenge to us.

Next morning it was as high as ever with big-muscled swells of roily strength pouring down a U-shaped bed. My saddle horse, who never refused a command, turned when his first step into it took the water to his knees, questioning if I really wanted to make the crossing. But he went on at my urgings and in two steps we were being carried downstream, mane and tail floating out with the current. We were swept down from the normal landing on the other side, past boulders and bushes, riding waist-deep in a giant grey roller coaster. Dream, who had decided that her place was immediately behind the lead horse, plunged in immediately behind and floated down with us. Fifty yards downstream we found bottom and floundered out on the far side.

Back at the crossing site Ruth drove Hash and O'Hara into the stream, fastened the reins of her mount so they wouldn't tangle and drove him in, too. Then she crawled over on a tree that had fallen across the stream a few yards above. At the next fording place we searched out a more favourable crossing.

Near the top of the pass a cabin surrounded by grass seemed a strategic place to stop. Our outfit was soaked and we expected a struggle with snow over the pass and with water down Smuts Creek on the other side. The cabin, smelly with the droppings of a hundred squirrels and rats and the remains of a porcupine behind the door, extended no welcome, but we borrowed the tin stove and set it up in the doorway of our tent to dry our belongings.

Surprisingly, we found the pass next morning free of snow. Also Smuts showed every sign of having moved out its spring quota of water so that our only discomfort in descending to the Spray River was the weather, lowering from the west, ghosting out the peaks and sprinkling rain on us all afternoon.

A packhorse bridge across the Spray River just below its junction with the Smuts was a welcome sight. Without it we would have had to swim the considerable flood of the Spray in order to get to Assiniboine. But as we approached it we saw a pole across from rail to rail, prohibiting passage. Did this mean the bridge was

The Upper Spray River and Spray Falls are beautiful, but Ruth and Cliff's campsite here is rained out.

Beautiful, turquoise Moraine Lake is nestled among the peaks not far from Lake Louise.

unsafe, should not be used? A hole about a foot wide showed in the deck where a puncheon had fallen away. Maybe the bar was up as a warning about this. Maybe it was simply to keep horses from wandering.

We looked the situation over, decided the bridge was by far the lesser of two risks and led three of the horses, one at a time, across it. The next one was to be O'Hara, an equine Doubting Thomas who preferred to pick his own way through difficulties on the trail and who sometimes went into mad spasms of pulling back and really trusting no one. Now at the sight of the foot-wide hole in the bridge he balked emphatically, pulled back savagely, jerked away and started a determined trot back-trail. Intercepting with my mount, I tried repeatedly to push him onto the bridge only to have him break away each time and run along the river bank, either upstream or down. Finally my urgings seemed to break his will. Standing momentarily on the bank, he whinnied a pathetic farewell to the horses across the river, and, instead of crossing the bridge, plunged into the flood. While we watched in dismay, he floated a quarter of a mile downstream, the pack buoying him up. He finally found footing, got ashore, and shedding water like a surfacing submarine, nickered a note of relief as he trotted up to rejoin his companions.

A mile up the trail Spray Falls was a beautiful sight, with acres of wonderful grass in front of it for the horses. But the meadow was half-flooded with spring runoff, so we pitched our tent beside a stream on the nearest high ground that was sufficiently level.

It was a miserable camp. A downpour of rain let loose as we unpacked, so we hastily erected the tent and threw our stuff inside. The fire we made with wet wood filled our little shelter with acrid smoke, driving Ruth to stick her head out frequently for relief. The tent leaked, and we went to bed in blankets half-soaked because of O'Hara's swim.

And in the dark of a very dark night, a porcupine came in and began chewing things to pieces. We knew it was a porcupine. We could hear its snuffling breathing and the swishing rattle of its quills.

Of all nature's creatures the porcupine seems to me to be the most unnecessary, and its presence in the scheme of things the cruellest. Although it cannot throw its quills, it can drive them with its heavy slashing tail into a steer's leg, a dog's face or a horse's tender muzzle. Once the tip of the quill is inserted, even a fraction of an inch, any movement, even an involuntary skin twitch, will work it ever deeper, causing slow and painful death to the victim.

Once when Neil MacKay and I had been stranded on foot with scant supplies near the top of MacArthur Pass, high in the Lake O'Hara country, we had come upon a miner deep in the mountains living on porcupine while waiting for his partner to return from town with supplies. We had given him most of our food. Two days later, in high broken plateau country, our horses had left us. After three days of searching we decided we ourselves had better leave for civilization and supplies. With only a light pack and a coil of rope we found a cabin in the rainy dusk, and without fire, utilized the cabin's only furniture, which was a pile of moss in one corner. We lay fully clothed in the moss, covering ourselves with it, lying close

Cliff's old friend, packer Neil MacKay, was with him when the two were terrorized by a marauding porcupine that tried to chew the boots off Cliff's feet.

enough to share each other's warmth and using the packsack and coil of rope for pillows. We had no way of blocking the doorway, as there was no door.

About dawn I was awakened by something chewing on my boots, which were still on my feet. Jackknifing with a shout, I woke Neil and we both saw a porcupine waddle out of the cabin into the forest. We discovered that from the pack under my head, the beast had hauled and liberally chewed some letters and a folded map while, almost under Neil's face, it had chewed the coiled rope into three or four pieces. If either of us had flung out an arm or even turned a head, a summer caper would have turned into a lifelong tragedy.

Two days before, we had killed a porcupine in an effort to stave off starvation, and as Neil said, it tasted like spruce bark and was so tough you couldn't stick a fork in the gravy.

Now here was another in the tent with Ruth and me, chewing, chewing. In the pitch-black night we couldn't go banging around with a club chasing a porcupine. We shouted. The chewing stopped, then started again. We shouted again, and it stopped again, started again, interminably. A flashlight would have been worth a hundred pounds of sugar but we didn't have one. Chew, chew, chew, whether we shouted or not. We lit a candle and the chewing stopped. We let the candle burn and slept until dawn.

Morning brought spotty sunshine and a drying breeze. We hung our blankets to dry and assessed the costs of the porcupine's visit: saddles chewed, latigoes cut in two, a bag of beans scattered about, boots chewed and a pair of fancy beaded gloves either eaten or carried away. Ruth would have to go bare-handed henceforth. Maybe there was more than one porcupine.

The trail we followed from the crossing of the Spray yesterday was one of the oldest in the Rockies, having been used by James Sinclair in 1841 when he took his first party to Oregon through White Man Pass. Four years after Sinclair, Father de Smet, the pioneering Belgian missionary, came from the Columbia via White Man Pass and down the Spray to deliver a message of peace to the Blackfoot Indians.

Pioneering Belgian missionary Father de Smet journeyed down the Spray River in 1845 to deliver a message of peace to the Blackfoot nation.

A few miles along this route we departed from it and tunnelled under gathering storm clouds up Bryant Valley. The morning's weather reprieve had been emphatically cancelled.

The warden's cabin at the junction of the Bryant Creek and Marvel Lake trails was locked, a mute suggestion that we keep going. The Marvel Lake trail would have led us through a remarkably beautiful corner of the Rockies over Wonder Pass to Mount Assiniboine. The pass was high, above timberline, and almost certain to be plugged with snow, so we stayed with Bryant Creek. Sometimes we were stirrup-deep in snowmelt and were always accompanied by a melancholy dirge of rasping and rattling as scabs of loose bark on burnt-out trees flapped in the wind. Churning clouds hid the peaks above. A 10-minute dash of rain came down and then a snow barrage as we took the sharp climb up the chimney of Assiniboine Pass itself. The snowflakes stuck where they landed, turning our horses white except for their eyes and nostrils and Ruth into a snow-girl with snow piling up on her eyelashes.

And that was the way of our entry into British Columbia on June 26 over the 7,152-foot Assiniboine Pass.

Beyond the actual portal we climbed even more, coming upon residual snow and horse tracks. When we gained the top of a long slope and could look down on Lake Magog and what the clouds revealed of Mount Assiniboine and the neighbouring peaks, we decided to camp amid the snowdrifts. A dry area under some alpine spruce took the tent, and while the horses foraged industriously toward the lake, we melted snow for cooking.

In one of the cabins near the lake we saw lamplight, and noted several other horses. We spent a pleasant evening and a restful night, untroubled by marauding porcupines or man-eating mosquitoes.

Mount Assiniboine, 11,870 feet, is the highest peak in the Canadian Rockies south of Banff, and towers almost 2,000 feet above its neighbours. Pointing skyward like a giant beacon, it can be seen from White Man Pass (Father de Smet mentioned it in his journals) and from the peaks surrounding Lake Louise.

Mount Assiniboine towers almost 2,000 feet above its neighbours.

Because it was there and was the biggest, it drew mountain climbers of renown from all over the world. They were often men of superb skill and accomplishment, but invariably referred to themselves as amateurs and to their paid guides (who had to be a combination of cowboy, cook, farrier, packer and axeman) as professionals.

The first man to scale Mount Assiniboine was a Church of England vicar, James Outram, later to become Sir James Outram. That was in 1901.

His mountain guide to the shores of Lake Magog, in the shadow of the huge peak, was Bill Peyto, who shared with most of his kind a reputation for reliability, proficiency and profanity, and there must have been a hundred times a day when Bill, coping with the packhorses, had to exercise unnatural verbal restraint out of respect for the vicar.

Other attempts at the mountain ending in disaster or death, along with its physical resemblance to the European peak, gave it the name of the Canadian Matterhorn.

Mount Eon, a neighbouring peak immediately to the south of Assiniboine rose to a similar level of deadly distinction in 1921.

It was on July 15 that Dr. Winthrop E. Stone, president of Purdue University, Lafayette, Indiana, accompanied only by his wife, virtually completed the first ascent of Mount Eon, 10,860 feet high, and then seconds later plunged to his death. Only minutes before, within a few feet of the top, he had left his wife while he climbed to reconnoitre. His wife saw him hurtling through the air and braced herself to stop his fall, for she believed they were still roped together. But when no shock came on the rope she realized he must have untied it. Without food, for the pack containing it had been carried by her husband, and inadequately clothed for a protracted stay on the mountain, she started the long climb down. In two days she descended about 2,000 feet, then became trapped on a narrow ledge. Here she was forced to stay until her rescue eight days after the accident.

Her survival was a triumph over the harshest of conditions. The only water available was two trickles of seepage, which she collected by digging under each a little basin. From these she was able to get a swallow of water every four hours, and to do this she disciplined herself and timed her drinking with her wristwatch. Every night she suffered from the cold and every day she recovered with the warmth of the sun — she was fortunate to be on the south side of the mountain — and constantly she faced the terrors of loneliness, starvation, bereavement (for she must have been certain her husband had been killed) and ebbing strength, until she was rescued.

It was through this corridor, near Lake Gloria and its mighty neighbours south of Mount Assiniboine, that Dr. Winthrop Stone and his wife travelled. He died in a fall after ascending Mount Eon, 10,860 feet, and his wife was rescued eight days later.

The people who rescued her and found her husband's body erected a cairn on the summit of Mount Eon, and on the top of the cairn, pointing skyward, they set Doctor Stone's ice axe.

Through the night the mountains had thrown off their cloud mantle and as we peered from our tent in the early morning, the sun, still unseen behind the eastern mountains, was sending tentative rays to tint in glowing pink a few remaining fleecy clouds and the long plume streaming out from the peak. As the sun rose the colour spilled from cloud to peak and while we watched, it flowed down over transverse layers of rock and ridges of snow onto supporting ice masses and hanging glaciers, dispelling the purples and greys from canyon and moraine until even Lake Magog, half-water, half-white ice, shone in the morning sun.

We had indeed seen Assiniboine!

A rider came up from the cabins by the lake. It was Bob Oleson, a friend of mine from Banff, whose party had come in a week ago. They had done lots of skiing but hadn't seen the sun or the mountain until this morning. This was their last day here and they were going to Kananaskis Lakes "if there wasn't too much snow." They were going to try Wonder Pass, high above the timberline over which all those involved in the Stone drama had passed.

We moved out at noon and dropped down through the Valley of the Rocks, which looked as if legendary giants had had a violent disagreement and thrown boulders at each other. The ground was dotted with pools of water from melting snow, and frequently we ran into bad trouble with fallen timber when avoiding these little lakes. At one lake edge we found fresh tracks of shod horses. A huge slide of rock crashed down unseen on the high slopes above us. The thunder of its brief existence lasted much longer than the slide, echoing from peak to peak, and the sulphurous smell of burnt rock carried to us by the breeze indicated that the slide was not far.

In Simpson Valley, under Citadel Pass, we came onto a camp of three men who had come up the Simpson River to hunt bear. They had a veritable village of two tents, a teepee and piles of equipment covered with canvas.

27

Despite their warning of fallen timber immediately ahead, we did not accept an invitation to spend the night in their camp. Just out of sight of their camp, we jumped into a mess of windfall through which we really earned our passage. We were led astray by sets of blazes that led nowhere and held up by having to extricate a packhorse or two who had insisted on doing their own trail finding. Finally, dog-tired, we camped in the last light of day on a patch of grass near the roaring Simpson River.

Overhead, clouds pink in the sunset came piling in from the west, suggesting that this morning's smile of sunshine might not be repeated. High above these, a layer of herringbone vapours picked up and held the sunset colours after the lower cloud had turned grey, and the shadows of the valley floor had ringed our little camp with curtains of black velvet.

Tomorrow we would go back into Alberta, over the continental divide by way of Simpson Pass. There would be no snow, we thought, since there had not been any to speak of on Assiniboine Pass, which was 200 feet higher. And, too, Simpson Pass shouted history, for it was through there that Sir George Simpson crossed the Rockies in his historic dash around the world in 1841. The guide back at the bear-hunting camp had said there would be fallen timber across the trail because no one had been over it this spring.

It was late when we went to bed, but we were up at five. The sky was overcast and threatening rain, and the horses, not liking the grass we had found them, preferred to back-trail and get trapped in the fallen timber. Their extrication and packing took longer than it should, so that we weren't on the trail until after ten.

Several timber-choked miles down the Simpson River we turned to the right on the trail leading to the pass. Some old cabins appeared beside the trail, one of them occupied by a pair of porcupines. "I wonder if they have a family," Ruth said. "How do they mate?"

I didn't know. I wished they wouldn't.

Fallen timber ceased to be a hindrance, but we came shortly to snow, getting deeper as we climbed. Because of it we lost the trail

The packhorse outfit rests at the top of Simpson Pass near Banff on June 28. A cairn marks the top of the continental pass between Alberta and British Columbia.

several times and plunged and floundered, and the horses began showing signs of fatigue. Residual snow left from the preceding winter is extremely inconsistent in its holding powers, so that progress over it or through it is always a falling, floundering, exhausting struggle. We rested the horses frequently and worked from tree to tree where the snow was shallower, prayed that our animals would not give up and were tremendously relieved to come

29

out on a hump-backed willowy meadow from which the snow had blown or melted partly clear. On the apex of the hump a small concrete-and-brass monument stated this was Simpson Pass, 6,954 feet high. I took a picture of the outfit, the clouds only a few feet above. The rain that dripped from some of the horses would find its way to the Pacific Ocean, while that from the others would go to Hudson's Bay.

Ruth smiled from the exact ridgepole of the continent.

Now our problem was to get back to summertime. A sign on a tree on the edge of this tundra patch warned us to be careful of fire. We deduced the trail should go down close to this sign, and for the next tense half-hour we walked rocky ridges, fell, slipped, scrambled, judged and misjudged and by the grace of God and my horse's super trail-brain, found the path under our feet when we got below the snow line. It had taken us four hours to cross the pass, a horizontal distance of about two miles.

We came to a cabin in about a quarter of a mile beside Healy Creek and saw it had a stove, table and bunk and was surrounded by forage. We were wet, tired and hungry, so we looked only for resident porcupines and finding none, we moved in.

As we unpacked and looked back up the mountain, we saw the snowy summit almost black under low cloud and shivered; we knew that not even our horses would wander from this little green paradise to go over that again. We turned them loose with only a bell and drag ropes.

Next morning, when the rain was pouring down and the horses comfortably resting under trees, we shed the cares of the trail and enjoyed the comforts of a stove and a cabin, even if the roof did leak.

Our predecessor, Hudson's Bay Company governor Sir George Simpson, would have been disgusted with us. The "Little Emperor" had a consuming passion for efficiency and speed. Starting from Fort Garry on July 3, 1841, at five o'clock in the morning, the party averaged 11 hours per day in the saddle and 50 miles. East of Edmonton the party overtook Sinclair's first Oregon-bound entourage, 23 families including 123 men, women and children. Simpson, under whose authority the emigrants were moving westward, stopped long enough to give the party a drink of rum, his blessings and instructions to go the regular route through the mountains by way of Athabasca Pass. Then, mounting fleet horses, he left Sinclair's plodding oxen far behind.

(Sinclair fell in with Chief Mackipictoon, who dissuaded him from using the northern Athabasca Pass and conducted him very successfully this first time through White Man Pass.)

At Edmonton, Simpson hired the half-Cree guide Peechee, who took them into the mountains by way of Devil's Head, and the north side of Lake Minnee-wan-kah, the Lake Where Spirits Dwell, the Devil's Lake of the white men. The Bow River was crossed near Banff and the party climbed Healy Creek to Simpson Pass and thence to the Columbia River, where boats waited to take them to Fort Vancouver.

The Little Emperor demanded speed. Sometimes the party with its 42 head of horses travelled eight hours before stopping for breakfast. On one occasion Simpson had his men out at one o'clock in the morning to gather in the horses that they might make their usual dawn start.

In the Banff area a day's halt was grudgingly called because it was discovered after eight hours' ride that six of the packhorses were missing. Camp was set up and men dispatched to look for the animals. They returned with the missing beasts at six the next morning whereupon the party continued its journey.

So the records tell us. Maybe the men, driven at such a mad rate, contrived a day's rest by tying up six of the horses that carried the most delectable foods for the governor, then reporting their absence eight hours later. Volunteering to return and search for the missing beasts, they would no doubt have sampled the goodies and enjoyed a rest. Maybe they detained the horses only an hour or so before reporting the loss. It seems impossible that an outfit travelling under the efficient scrutiny of Sir George would even start, let alone travel for eight hours, without someone knowing where each horse was.

Our speed was probably closer to Sinclair's than Simpson's, but the day's stopover cured the weather and invigorated us all, and the following morning we dropped briskly down a good trail beneath Simpson Pass, down Healy Creek to Brewster Creek and the Bow River. Rather than going downstream to Banff, we ascended the Bow and came by late afternoon to Redearth Creek, which brawled out of the mountains.

There we camped in a grove of sibilant poplars and were attended by immense mosquitoes and joyfully singing robins.

Bath Creek, up against Kicking Horse Pass, received its name because the famous but impetuous Major Rogers was too impatient to camp overnight by a swollen glacial stream. Spurring his horse into the water, he was promptly upset and might have drowned had not his companion, Tom Wilson, pulled him out with a pole. They camped by the stream until next morning and made a safe crossing. In later years, when the stream was running high and dirty from glacial melting, railway crews working down valley would remark, "The old man must be having another bath."

Our passage of Redearth Creek next morning was unexciting.

It was July 1, Ruth's birthday, and we hoped to be at Lake Louise to party with her folks. We suffered delay investigating alluring trails that led us where we didn't want to go, crossed to the north side of the Bow on the Vermilion Pass bridge, and, borrowing highway and railway rights of way, put miles quickly behind us. A black storm drove down, frigid winds buffeted us, and darkness made it necessary to camp within only five miles of Lake Louise station. Unlike Sir George Simpson we would not travel in the dark.

Next morning we got our outfit out on the highway, where we presented an attraction for motoring tourists almost equal to a bear or a moose alongside the road. We were overjoyed to be discovered by Ruth's folks, travelling in a pickup truck. We were almost a day late in arriving.

At our camp that day, great piles of food appeared out of the truck and were eaten. Adventures of the last two weeks were told and retold, and all admired Ruth's quickly acquired horsemanship.

No mention was made of the difficulties or possible dangers ahead, unless they all were reflected in the brief conversation between Ruth and Hamish Guthrie, a young Scot who said to her in his soft burr, "Ach, Ruth, my girl, suppose you take this seat and go back to Calgary, and I'll go with Cliff to yon ocean?"

And Ruth smiled as she shook her head and replied, "Thanks, but no!"

When they had gone, we walked over to a tree and there, chopping out a smooth blaze, we inscribed over our signatures our resolution: BELLA COOLA OR BUST.

In the months to come there were indeed times of doubt regarding the outcome.

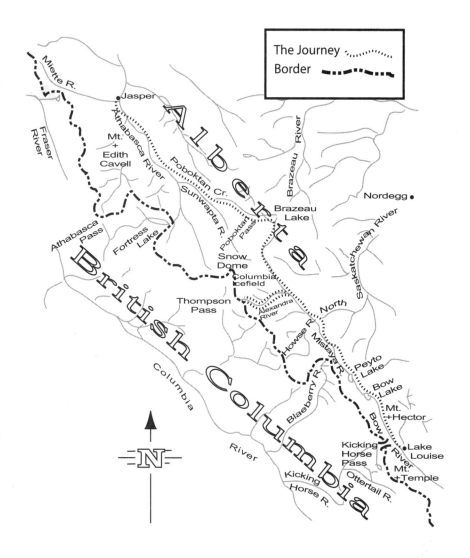

The Journey ∙∙∙∙∙∙∙∙∙∙
Border ▬∙▬∙▬∙▬

Miette R.

Fraser River

Jasper

Mt. + Edith Cavell

Athabasca River

Alberta

Poboktan Cr.

Sunwapta R.

Poboktan Pass

Brazeau River

Brazeau Lake

Nordegg •

Athabasca Pass

Fortress Lake

British Columbia

Snow Dome

Columbia Icefield

Saskatchewan River

Thompson Pass

Alexandra River

Howse R.

North

Columbia

Blaeberry R.

Mistaya R.

Peyto Lake

Bow Lake

Mt. + Hector

River

Kicking Horse Pass

Bow River

Lake Louise

—N—

Kicking Horse R.

Ottertail R.

Mt. + Temple

LAKE LOUISE TO JASPER

For two days we rode the trails around Lake Louise. We climbed to the top of the larger of the two Beehives, and looked down on the Lakes in the Clouds, and on Louise, which lay like a turquoise teardrop. We struggled along the steep trails of Paradise Valley to the Giant Steps, where Paradise Creek tumbles over huge rocks and throws upon each a veil of filmy spray. We found that all trails at Lake Louise pointed skyward, as if drawing attention to the massive glaciers and the five great peaks that looked down upon our neighbours of only 10,000 feet. (They were Mount Temple, 11,636 feet; Mount Victoria, 11,365 feet; Mount Lefroy, 11,230 feet; Mount Hungabee, 11,457 feet; and Mount Huber, 11,051 feet.)

We learned that Lake Louise Station is the third name for the train depot there. Following the building of the Canadian Pacific Railway it was for some years known as Laggan, and before that, during construction days, Holt City.

We learned also that while the Indians used Kicking Horse Pass in coming from the Columbia and Kootenay valleys, they avoided the heavy canyon country by coming up the Ottertail River and MacArthur Creek to MacArthur Pass and Lake O'Hara, thence down Cataract Creek to the actual pass.

North of Lake Louise the Bow Valley continues, offering a pleasant open door to the northern mountain section, only slightly obstructed by muskeg, fallen timber and sometimes a sudden fluctuation in altitude. Twenty-five packhorse-miles north of Lake

Near Lake Louise, Paradise Creek tumbles down the Giant Steps with Mount Ringrose in the background.

Louise the trail climbs over Bow Pass, 6,878 feet, and drops into the Mistaya Valley, then down to meet the North Saskatchewan River. Then it ascends to the Big Hill and Sunwapta Pass, 6,675 feet, where it enters the Arctic watershed and follows the Sunwapta and Athabasca rivers to Jasper. Because the Rockies consist of several parallel ranges and some not so parallel, there are alternate routes, but the Bow-North Saskatchewan-Athabasca River route is considered the trunk highway. In its entire length, the series of valleys makes an Albertan parallel to the Rocky Mountain trench of British Columbia, except that it is half the length and is blocked with two high passes — not geographically so remarkable but affording footing for spectacular trails.

White man's first exploratory thrusts into the western mountains took him north of this region when Alexander Mackenzie ascended the Peace River in 1793. The next took him to the very centre of it with David Thompson's use of the North Saskatchewan approach and Howse Pass from 1807 to 1810. When it was desirable to bypass the Piegan warriors, Thompson went north again and in 1811 explored and developed the Athabasca Pass route, which was to remain the highway for the fur trade until the use of ships on the Pacific Coast lessened the importance of any overland route.

In the late 1850s and early 1860s, the gravels of the North Saskatchewan were sifted by gold seekers, but rewards were insufficient to draw crowds.

In the 1870s the same gravels crunched under the tread of railway explorers investigating the North Saskatchewan–Howse Pass route as a possibility for the Canadian Pacific Railway.

But the railway came up the Bow Valley only as far as Laggan (now Lake Louise Station), then diverged towards the totally new Kicking Horse Pass. Its advent made Banff and Laggan the outfitting and departure points for adventurous trips into the far wilderness. Packhorse trails radiated from them to Assiniboine in the south, to Robson in the northwest and to a hundred hidden mountains in between. After the railways were built through Jasper and the Yellowhead, trips were considered outstanding if they extended across the gap from railway to railway, or "steel to steel."

One of the most amazing alternatives to the main trail led across a corner of the Columbia Icefield (into the Ice Age and out again) and was travelled with horses. This trail was pioneered in 1921 by a party that included Dr. J. Munroe Thorington, author of several books on climbing in the Canadian Rockies and Selkirks, Dr. William Ladd, also a noted alpinist, alpine guide Conrad Kain, mountain guide Jimmy Simpson and cook and horse wrangler Ulysses La Casse.

The trail led up the Alexandra River, to Castleguard Meadows on the southwest side of the Columbia Icefield, then onto the ice itself and down the long reach of the Saskatchewan Glacier, from its snout to the main trail.

The actual crossing of the ice is tersely told by Dr. Thorington in his 1925 book, *The Glittering Mountains of Canada*:

> The ultimate sources of the Castleguard River head in a low divide with meadows, which we crossed to a tiny marginal lake by the Saskatchewan Glacier, nearly opposite Mount Athabasca. A shore of flat moraine permitted the pack train to progress to level ice. Our horses on the glacier made an unusual procession; but, at first timid, they soon became accustomed to their surroundings and, like true mountaineers, hopped over the little cracks and crevasses. It was necessary, in avoiding a lateral glacier entering from the south, to take to the central ice for a short distance. The horses were taken down the glacier for more than four miles, with devious winding around the large transverse crevasses. The steep terminal moraine, with treacherously balanced boulders and slippery glacial mud, was most troublesome, requiring some trail-building and considerable care to avoid damage to the pack train. But before evening the last horse was safely off and camp finally made below the tongue on the flats toward the south side near a pleasant waterfall.

Close by, the stream enters a narrow canyon, spanned by a natural bridge; apparently no one else, with horses, had ever stopped at our Glacier Camp.

The hydrographic apex of the Columbia Icefield — called "The Mother of Rivers," by Lewis Freeman in his 1925 article of the same name in the *National Geographic Magazine* is the Snowdome, 11,340 feet high, and this mountain wrings tribute from the clouds and sends water back to three of the world's oceans. Streams born out of its glaciers join the Columbia to flow into the Pacific on the west, through the Saskatchewan River system and Hudson Bay to the North Atlantic on the east, and finally a third lot flows through the Athabasca and Mackenzie rivers into the Arctic Ocean.

The Alberta–British Columbia Boundary Commission in 1919 and 1920 collated the information of various trail-makers, and, with instrument surveys, established what through here was the hydrographic divide as well as the interprovincial boundary.

With the establishment and extension of the national parks, wardens broadened trails, built bridges, restrained poachers and occasionally conducted or assisted in rescue operations.

When the stock market crash and the Hungry Thirties brought distress to millions and governments sought to create make-work programs, one project undertaken was the building of a highway from Lake Louise to Jasper. Work started in 1931 and was labour-oriented rather than machine-powered and hundreds of men got jobs. Pay was minimal, as little as 50 cents per day, but the food was good and plentiful and the roomy tents were better than the open ground in Turner Valley, which was sometimes shared with dogs and pigs.

It was washday activity at Lake Louise that brought us to the attention of the park warden. Ruth insisted that our clothes needed washing so an extra large fire was built and the clothes were boiling merrily over it when a pickup truck bearing Parks insignia on the door drove up. A man stepped out, looked the situation over, saw the pile of horse gear and told us to be careful of fire. When I asked him his name he said he was La Casse.

The name was electrifying. La Casse! Guide, cook, packer, mountain man: as such he had become legendary. At least twice he had crossed from Castleguard Meadows down the Saskatchewan Glacier with a pack train. I fired questions so rapidly that he smiled and invited us to his home for the evening. There, over a table covered with maps he offered valuable information on mountain trails. "Nasty crossing here. Don't pass up this grass ... there isn't any for the next 12 miles. This map is mistaken here. Look, these two contradict each other. It's real trouble when a mistake ever gets on a map. Harder to get off than warts."

Could we take our small outfit down the Saskatchewan Glacier?

"It's too early in the season. Snow-bridges aren't melted yet and you couldn't tell where the crevasses are. You have to wind back and forth across the ice and one error could cost you your outfit ... in a minute. The first crossing took us 11 hours, long enough for a snowstorm to come up and wipe you out ... But that Alexandra River country and Castleguard is worth going for a look."

Three nights later Dr. Thorington (*the* Dr. Thorington) and Jim Simpson (*the* Jim Simpson) were telling us the same at Bow Lake.

Warden La Casse had told us that they had gone in, Mrs. Thorington accompanying them, two days before. Ruth and I had left our Lake Louise camp at noon of July 5 and taken the newly built road pointing toward Jasper. We saw the road deteriorate from good gravel to dirt to a wagon road and finally to a muddy pack-trail. Mount Temple sank behind us, Mount Hector lifted in rocky eminence on our right and hard over on the left, Hector Lake caught the late afternoon sun. Evening and a swampy pasture for the horses coincided and we stopped for the night.

The evening was clear and too cold for mosquitoes. Instead of erecting the tent we rolled it out and made our bed on it. With two canvas-wrapped rocks from the fire for foot-warmers and the

Cliff and Ruth get ready to leave Lake Louise.

stars twinkling close above, it was a comfortable and memorable camp. In the lonesome depth of dusk, a train flashed like a giant firefly down on the tracks near Lake Louise and its wailing echoed through the valleys and peaks as it rushed through the wilderness forest to some distant Pacific rendezvous. We felt childishly happy and secure in our cocoon of canvas.

The next morning everything was crackling white with frost and we wasted no time breaking camp.

That afternoon the bottle-green claw of Crowfoot Glacier holding a mountain in its clasp showed as we went around Bow Peak. Then the azure waters of Bow Lake smiled at us. Beyond the lake to our left, glaciers rose to snowfields that swept over the horizon, while to the right grassy meadows led to the low skyline of Bow Pass. Bow Lake is 6,500 feet high and the pass, some six or seven miles distant, is only 378 feet higher, a broad open invitation to farther mountain travels.

Jim Simpson, with the whole of the west to choose from 30-odd years ago, had decided this was the best. On the shores of the lake only yards from where the little stream born on Bow Pass entered it, he had built a permanent camp of logs. The main building was a many-sided blockhouse with a huge fireplace of native stone, and it was from this building that he stepped when we rode up. Blue-eyed, moustached, he studied us for several seconds before his expression turned to one of welcome.

While we were erecting our tent, a doe appeared on the trail and watched us; then she bounded away and returned with three more, who seemed equally interested in what we were doing. Then they were gone, as suddenly as they had come.

That night we visited with the Simpsons. Jim's young son, Jimmy, was with him, and Dr. Thorington and his wife. The doctor's speech was not quite as terse as his written language but just as full of information, and Jim Simpson, veteran of more than 30 years of trail making, trail riding and dude wrangling, was voluble and entertaining. Right now his anger was directed at a trio from Calgary who had used one of his cabins without permission and left it in a filthy mess.

"Do they live like that, like pigs, in Calgary?" he demanded.

He told us of amusing things that had happened on the trail: of a guide who spent a long morning looking for the 15th horse in the outfit, for instance. Fourteen he could find, but not the 15th, until someone pointed out that he was riding it. And some not so funny, such as the time a dude wanted to cut a fishing line. Jim handed him his pet axe, sharp as a razor, and as precious to a guide as the roping-horse is to the cowboy performer.

"I was speechless when, instead of drawing his line across the sharp blade, he stepped over to a rough boulder, laid the line across it and chopped. Second try was successful but I hadn't yet recovered my power of speech."

He gave us a lash rope and hooked cinch for our packs and told us that if there was anything else we needed, Dr. Thorington would hunt it out of camp supplies and give it to us. Boats and fishing tackle were ours to be used when we liked, but when we offered to take him part way to Lake Louise (his horses had backtracked) he refused the offer saying it would be "too much trouble." It might be a 25-mile-hike to Lake Louise. "Nothing at all," he said. Truly, as Dr. Thorington stated, the Indians had nicknamed him well, "the Wolverine," for the speed he travelled mountain trails.

I asked about crossing the ice with horses.

"Don't try taking the horses out onto the ice," Simpson said. "It takes an outfit with quite a few men and a lot of study. It's like spending a winter. The edges look a long way away if your cache of food has been raided by a wolverine in the middle of it. But that Castleguard is the easiest way to get to the icefield. And you get a view like looking out of an upstairs window!"

It was midnight and brilliant moonlight when we blew out the candle after writing mail to send with the Simpsons in the morning. But we did not sleep immediately, for hardly had the glowing wick of the candle died out than our tent ropes were struck by something, and great shadows played on the canvas. Tall creatures rose up and sparred in pantomime, and we heard a sound of clicking in the midnight air, almost like castanets. The play went on for several minutes, while cloven hooves kicked the canvas and rapped the ropes. Then we saw the outline of a deer's rump, a flick of its tail, and the performance was over.

Simpson had told us the deer often came up on the porch of his cabin and looked in the door. They licked our saddles and were always around, peering, studying. Once they helped me find the horses. I would have walked by without seeing them had not a deer, peering into the willows, led me to investigate. There were the horses, lying so quietly that the bell was silent.

We stayed for three full days at Bow Lake. The first morning, after saying goodbye to the Simpsons, we offered the use of two of our horses to the Thoringtons, who were going to hike to Bow Pass. They refused the horses with thanks, saying they preferred to walk. I was amazed and said so to Ruth, back at camp. It was the first time I had ever met anyone who preferred to walk 10 or 12 miles rather than ride.

We borrowed a rowboat and tackle and went fishing. Delightfully lazy, we rowed to the lower end of the lake, ate our lunch under

Beautiful Bow Lake, beside the snowy slopes of the Crowfoot Glacier, is home for three blissful days.

the claws of Crowfoot Glacier, and nearly caught a fish. Got back to the Simpson cabin as the Thoringtons returned from their 12-mile stroll and received an invitation from them to spend the evening there.

It was the first of several visits. They fed us huge quantities of bannock and cocoa, and introduced us to the practice of using small bowls instead of mugs.

"It saves frequent calls for repeats," the doctor said.

We also learned from him that practically all of the glaciers of the Rockies were receding and that the term "glacier" was a general term which had four modifiers: hanging, alpine, parasitic and piedmont; that the advance and recession of glaciers is cyclic and depends on six different factors, that crevasses are caused by the ice travelling faster in the centre than along the edges; that the centre moraine is created by two ice floes joining and carrying their moraines jointly; that mountains were sometimes massifs, that they had faces, names and characters.

Both the doctor and Jim Simpson had spoken of the picturesque territory at the head of Bow Lake, and there we found canyons, one with a boulder acting as a natural bridge — awesome indeed. Bow Glacier, born out of the Waputick Icefield, in turn gave birth to a dirty, growling, tempestuous stream, another source of the Bow River. The Bow Glacier also warned us of coming rain when it turned black under clouds boiling in from the west. We got back to camp just ahead of the rain, which lasted all day, all night and all the next day.

We stayed over the rainy day doing our three "r's", writing, resting and repairing and the following morning gathered in our horses, said goodbye to our friends (Mrs. Thorington called Ruth "Pioneer Lady," with a soft look in her eyes), and directed our horses toward Bow Pass. We had the feeling somehow that we were just now leaving home with a whole, brand-new world ahead of us.

From a lookout the Thoringtons had told us about, we gained a tremendous view of the country ahead. The Mistaya River is born on the north side of Bow Pass and joins with the ice-green stream flowing out of Peyto Lake. Then the stream flows north, broadening into Mistaya Lake and the Waterfowl Lakes to create shining beads on a silvery string. Otherwise the valley of the Mistaya was filled with forest, on the bottom and up the sides, until glaciers and rocky pinnacles took over.

Almost under our feet and a little to the left, Peyto Glacier ground down the side of a mountain to send a half-dozen silt-laden streams of about a quarter-mile in length into Peyto Lake. The lake received the silty water, cleansed it and sent it down valley, where, away to the north, it flowed into the North Saskatchewan River.

A wind, as frigid as the snow it swept, had harassed us as we packed at Bow Lake. It had slapped us, sometimes on the back, sometimes in the face, as we rode toward the pass, and it now forced us with higher velocity and spitting rain to seek lower altitudes and the protection of timber.

We did not drop far, only to Peyto Lake, 6,102 feet, but the upper Mistaya Valley was breathlessly quiet and warm. The trees were not tall enough to shut out the views of the high mountains. The

The Mistaya River churns and foams through this narrow canyon before joining the combined Howse and North Saskatchewan rivers.

immense glacier-hung slopes of Mount Patterson gleamed above us on our left, while on the right, the almost unbroken massif made up of Cirque Peak, Observation Peak and Mount Weed presented a mosaic of brilliant colours as the sun came and went. We found a good camping site near the lower end of Mistaya Lake just where it seemed we would have to make a wet crossing of the Mistaya River. The stream was divided here into several turbulent channels on a wide gravel bottom, but it looked as if any one of them might require swimming.

We made a snug, comfortable camp, went fishing (no luck), came back and built a roaring fire. Next morning we discovered that a trail had been built on our side of the river, and no crossing was necessary.

We liked the name Mistaya. Dr. Thorington had sad it was Cree for grizzly bear. We didn't see any bears, but we did see placidly beautiful lakes, great walls of boulders cemented together in layers stacked on top of one another to make mountains ten and eleven thousand feet high, with an occasional narrow gap from which burst gushing streams, open forests and dark ones, too, with great pinnacles shining with light among the misty morning clouds.

Lower down, the Mistaya River plunges into a narrow, twisty canyon, in places only a few feet wide, through which it churns and foams, cutting big caverns in the rock before discharging its pale blue flood into the muddy surge of the combined Howse and North Saskatchewan rivers.

At almost the same spot where the Mistaya from the south meets the North Saskatchewan from the north, a third stream of about the same size, the Howse River, arrives from the west, and, under the name of the North Saskatchewan, flows out between two lofty peaks, Mount Murchison and Mount Wilson, to the prairies. Through this gateway, feathered warriors of the plains rode against their enemies, white traders moved with their trade goods and explorers searched for a way to the Pacific Ocean.

The first man treading this opening to be mentioned by historians was a mountain man, Jaco Finlay, who in 1806, at David

The gateway through Mount Murchison and Mount Wilson, formed where the Howse River (above) joins the North Saskatchewan from the west, was used by fur traders and by explorers searching for a route to the Pacific Ocean.

Thompson's orders, marked out the trail up the Howse River and over the pass used by the Kootenay Indians when they came over the mountains from the west to trade.

Then in 1807 David Thompson, fur trader, explorer and surveyor, came with his 22-year-old wife and their three children, the youngest a babe in arms, and camped on the banks of the Howse with his small party for two weeks to permit some of the snow to melt on the pass. On June 25 they climbed over the 5,010-foot summit (later to be called Howse Pass) and in five days reached the Columbia River, where the stream that they had followed down from the pass, the Blaeberry, entered it a few miles north of the present city of Golden.

They were lucky. The Piegans, who controlled the North Saskatchewan approach to the mountains, enjoyed a trade monopoly-cum-military superiority with the Indian people on the other side of the mountains because of trade goods and firearms they received from white traders. They had no thought of letting white men into the territory to supply them directly with these goods.

But in the spring of 1807 the tribal warriors were far south, warring against wagon trains on the Oregon Trail in an effort to avenge the death of two of their members who had fallen in a skirmish with the Lewis and Clark expedition.

In 1809 Joseph Howse, a clerk of the Hudson's Bay Company, started using the pass and it was given his name.

The Indians were not always absent, and they were so great a threat that Thompson sought a new pass. In the bitter winter of 1810 he took his men up the Whirlpool River over the 5,736-foot Athabasca Pass, which was under 20 feet of snow, and never suspected the existence of the little lake that drains to both Pacific and Atlantic (the one that Governor Simpson later named The Committee Punchbowl). Nor did he comment on Mount Brown or Mount Hooker, which flank the pass, as they were invisible in those weather conditions.

Howse Pass, with its constant threat of Indian attack, was abandoned and thousands of people and millions of dollars in trade goods and fur moved over Athabasca Pass in Thompson's footsteps.

Although Thompson explored and mapped 2 million square miles of wilderness, no pass that he trod bears his name, nor does any other geographical feature except the Thompson River, named by Simon Fraser, a river which Thompson never saw.

In 1858 Dr. James Hector made a trip over the Vermilion Pass and back over the Kicking Horse Pass, which he named thus in peculiar honour to his saddle horse, which kicked him in the chest and knocked him unconscious. He then came over Bow Pass and down the Mistaya, which he called the Little Fork of the Saskatchewan. Turning left at the forks he ascended the Howse and detoured to Glacier Lake. Above this he climbed to the Lyell Icefield. Then, returning to the North Saskatchewan River, he followed it out to Edmonton.

He came into the mountains a year later by way of the Bow and went up the Pipestone over the 8,000-foot pass to the Siffleur River. This he descended to its junction with the North Saskatchewan, and again turning left, ascended this stream and the Howse River. His guide, Nimrod, had deserted him, so Hector became his own guide, finding his way successfully through Howse Pass and down the Blaeberry to the Columbia River.

Twenty years later explorers and surveyors were examining the Bow Pass–Howse Pass–Blaeberry River section as a route for the Canadian Pacific Railway, and many were critical of Major A. B. Rogers for his choice of the Kicking Horse Pass instead.

Moose were far more numerous than men when we camped by the warden's cabin on the Howse River. Two moved out of the meadow as we approached and that evening another visited among our horses on a welcoming basis. Next morning when the sun came up through the Saskatchewan River gap east of us, we heard the sound of splashing, and, peering out of our tent, we saw two moose puddling in a shallow slough of the Howse. An unusually nice day seemed promised so we took lunches and cameras and climbed a sugar-loaf mound from which we could overlook the broad river bed and watch the moose crossing the three or four hurrying grey streams. We saw a dozen of the great beasts in two hours and when we made the crossing next morning we didn't even get stirrups wet, because the moose had marked out the shallowest route for us.

Another pleasant surprise awaited us: a bridge across the North Saskatchewan. Our map had shown no bridge on the Mistaya, no bridge on the Saskatchewan. La Casse had pointed out other errors, even contradictions in the maps.

"It's one less river to cross," sang Ruth as the horses clattered across the sturdy structure.

That afternoon we rode out on to the broad gravel bar where the Alexandra River flows in from the west to join the North Saskatchewan. This was our destination for the afternoon, for if we were to go to Castleguard Meadows, we would ascend the Alexandra River to where it changes its name as well as its direction, becomes the Castleguard, and plunges down from the north from Castleguard Meadows. This spot at the junction of the Alexandra and North Saskatchewan was Graveyard Camp, so

A bridge across the North Saskatchewan River, shown here near its source, means "one less river to cross," in Ruth's words.

named because it had been the gathering point for hunting parties who had picked over their trophies and left the rejects in the form of skulls and antlers hanging from trees. It was a good campsite.

Next morning we again tried to pack the colt, Hash, but she bolted as soon as we started to tighten the cinch for the packsaddle and went bucking and bawling across the gravel flats like a horse at the Calgary Stampede. After the second attempt we gave up. Rather than have her smash more of our precious camp supplies we would wait until we could use a dummy pack.

Fording the North Saskatchewan was easy, maybe due to cold weather or perhaps because we were so close to its source.

The map shows the trail up the Alexandra as being for the most part in the river, and in this case it was literally true. The Alexandra River is like the Howse, having a bed thrice as large as it needs except for times of freshet. Down this broad gravel bed it follows many courses. Deposits of glacial mud along the edges of the streams have provided anchorage and sustenance for grass, with which they

51

combine to build surprisingly firm but quite narrow ridges or atolls right on the brink of a deep, rushing stream. Sometimes the depth of the channels forced us into the woods, there to be challenged by torrents coming down from the ice caps of Mount Saskatchewan (10,964 feet), or by fallen timber or rocks.

On one of the brief interludes in the forest we met a pack train of six packhorses and four riders. Their headman was Innes (I didn't learn his first name) from Nordegg, over the mountains to the east, and their horses were all small. But what they lacked in size they made up in enthusiasm, for although the men were willing to stop and talk, the packhorses were more than eager to continue their journey. Each of them wore the galvanized screen nosebag farmers put on their horses in fly-time. The bag didn't hinder breathing or drinking, but it did keep the wearer from stopping for a nibble, and his mind on getting to the next campsite as soon as possible. The result was a good 25 percent increase in speed and efficiency, and saved wear on everybody's nerves. A wonderful investment.

The backdrop to our ascent of the Alexandra River was a wall of mountains: Mount Spring Rice (10,749 feet), Mount Fresnoy (10,730 feet) and Mount Alexandra (11,214 feet). They were all heavily glaciated, and they all watched with frigid disinterest as

The heavily glaciated mountains at the head of the Alexandra River prove to be as inhospitable as they appear.

The scenic splendour of Castleguard Falls is close to Castleguard Meadows, a natural balcony facing west that is Cliff and Ruth's home for two days.

we struggled towards them. Great clouds began boiling in from the west, and now and then there was a deep roll of thunder, so we made camp at the first suitable spot.

Our camp, close to where the Castleguard River changes its name to Alexandra, was Last Grass camp, and the commencement of a strenuous struggle with river, forest, old trail and new, a sharp detour around a narrow canyon, all made more adventurous by the river jumping from its bed to flood the forest. In one place we saw a spring of water, fully a foot in diameter, gushing straight up from the forest floor three feet high to create its own fountain, pool and stream. Then we came to where the Castleguard River plunges over a ledge to make a fine waterfall and join with Watchman Creek out of Thompson Pass to the west, preparatory to giving horse-travellers a lot of trouble downstream.

Starting within a quarter-mile of the falls, a steep but well-marked trail led us upward and soon we were on Castleguard Meadows, a natural balcony from which we could look westward past Watchman Peak into the Thompson Pass and British Columbia. The Bush Valley, beyond the pass, was dark with clouds and we turned to the brighter uplands and camped, as others had, beside a little brook marked by a few trees whose branches were all on one side because of the persistent down-drafts from the glaciers above.

Thompson Pass, 6,511 feet high, was not named after David Thompson, but after a C. S. Thompson who visited the area, with one packer, in the year 1900.

Castleguard Meadows was our home for two days. The first day, we tramped along the edge of the seemingly eternal snowbanks and bulges of ice that squeezed down from the snowy horizon. We found a walking route onto the glaciers that seemed to be the main constituent of Castleguard Mountain, and scrambled up over repeated ridges. A few boulders that had dropped off peaks further up offered us focal points in the otherwise vacant expanses of ice.

Castleguard Mountain, 10,096 feet, rises almost sheer on its west side to a chimney-like peak, but on the east side, which faces the icefield, it is banked with snow and ice and is the lookout point for a view of the icefield. We climbed to maybe 8,000 feet — we could only guess — and looked down onto the Saskatchewan Glacier, along which Simpson had repeatedly taken pack trains.

"Is it like that, down there?" Ruth asked, pointing to a nest of crevasses where flowing ice was inching over a deep-down shoulder of rock.

I nodded, and she made no further comment; her answer was to come that evening in camp.

Clouds had been filling in from the west and now a particularly black one reached down on us, so we took refuge behind a boulder for 15 minutes while snowflakes covered us and everything else.

It passed suddenly, and the world was a dazzling white as we descended quickly to the Meadows. Weather had not finished with us, however, for we were soon overtaken by wind-driven rain that came at us like miniature darts and made the shelter of our camp more than welcome.

As we crouched, wet and weary, and warmed ourselves by our fire, sheltered from the biting wind by only a piece of canvas, we knew we had had enough.

"They can have all the Swissing they want. I'm going to stick to horses and dirt trails," said Ruth.

Next day we rested, did camp chores, sharpened axes, and after a painfully cold night, even with rocks for foot warmers, we awoke to a sagging tent and four inches of snow over everything. We felt that the welcome mat of the alpine regions had generously been laid down for us, and that the Columbia Icefield was truly breathing a welcome down our necks. In flagrant lack of gratitude we packed our horses and dropped to lesser altitudes, fighting the obstructions of the lower Castleguard River, finding the Alexandra River a foot lower because of the cold weather and arriving in the course of time back at Graveyard Camp.

We found company there.

As we splashed out of the North Saskatchewan we saw people moving about in front of three white tents pitched among the trees. A big young man greeted us and asked if we planned on camping

55

there, and if so would we mind him helping unpack. Fifteen minutes after riding into camp our horses were free, had enjoyed their roll and were on their way to grass, and Ruth and I were sitting down to a cup of tea in the largest of the tents.

"Riviere is my name and George my handle," said the young giant. "And this is my wife, Maggie, and her sister Annie Clark." The two young women were not much bigger than Ruth (an even five feet) and about the same age. There were two men in the party besides George: Ray Cyrl and Slim Black. Slim was from Banff, the rest of the party from Waterton Lake.

The Rivieres were professional outfitters who had been in business in the Waterton area and were now en route to the Cariboo goldfields to start anew there, in the packing business. They had left Waterton on the 15th of May, followed the Alberta foothills north, and had gone through Kicking Horse Pass down to the Columbia River. They had hoped to follow this down to the Big Bend, then continue in a northerly direction up Canoe River. The trails had not been used for a score of years and were in a horrible state of disrepair. In 20 years the heavy precipitation of the steep Pacific slope, with rock and snow-slide, and the vigorous vegetation, had reclaimed the wilderness. They had bridged the torrent of Cummins Creek with a log, cutting down a tree with light camp axes, and led their horses across on that. They had attempted the Wood River, which leads to Fortress Lake, but there was no trail there and the canyon-torn country turned them back after two bruising weeks of effort. A month after they had gone through Kicking Horse Pass, they recrossed it and came up the Bow.

"We gave the snow in the passes a long time to melt," George grinned. Now they wanted to get to Quesnel and the goldfields with as little adventure as possible.

He suggested we travel together.

"We'll probably do enough to make good stories for you."

It would have been a solution to problems that we could not anticipate, but for the moment we planned travels in company only as far as Jasper. We wanted to see mountain country that might not lead by the shortest route to Quesnel.

George assumed the role of teacher-benefactor as well as trail companion. He taught us how to erect our tent with poles using only six feet of rope; he traded us bigger pack boxes because ours were too small. He ripped a seam in the roof of our tent, installed a roof plate made of a couple of fire-protection signs fastened together with brass rivets (of the kind used for harness work) and a hole cut in the centre large enough to accommodate small stovepipes. Then he gave us a set of telescoping stovepipes and a collapsible tin stove to fit neatly into our tent ... "for when it rains," he grinned, obviously pleased at our appreciation.

When he was told of our troubles with Hash, he said, "I'll pack her as long as we travel together. In a week or two she'll be a well-broken packhorse."

And in their biggest tent (the cook tent), he beat me three times out of three at cribbage. "I'm sure glad you came along," he said. "Everybody in my crew has beaten me so bad I began to think I didn't know how to play."

The packhorse in this picture is George Riviere, shown here with his outfit. The Rivieres, professional outfitters en route to the Cariboo goldfields, are good company and a great help to Ruth and Cliff on their way to Jasper.

Somehow or other fresh venison, tenderloin, appeared in their frying pans, and as we ate there were vague stories with reference to a deer that had been shot for raiding the warden's gardens. The nearest gardens were many, many miles away, and Slim and Ray parodied and sang a suggestive version of "Poachers on Parade," and as George finished his plate, he sighed.

"Next time I go to jail for shooting a deer out of season I am going to tell the warden every morning how good the venison was," he grinned, "and ask him if he wouldn't like a quarter of the next one I get."

Next morning ropes were strung taut between trees, creating a corral into which the horses were driven and held, to be taken out one at a time for packing. One of the young women stood by a pair of pack boxes to indicate the load to go on the next horse, and one of the men would bring up a packhorse, already saddled. Giving the lead rope to the waiting woman, he would start packing, with a second man on the other side. It took about 10 minutes from the time the horse was led to the pack until, its pack balanced, covered with canvas and lashed down with the diamond hitch, the young woman tied it to a tree to await departure. Frequently two horses were being packed at one time. Every move was made with the precision of long practice.

The packing of our rebellious horse, Hash, was left until the last. Two "hardware" boxes containing such almost indestructibles as horseshoes, hammers and camp axes, filled out with extra canvas and ropes and securely tied, were to be her burden, a heavy but compact pack, for the day. Now, mounting his horse, a sturdy animal with a heavy stock saddle on it, George snubbed Hash's head close to the saddle horn and Ray and Slim, wary and nimble-footed, blanketed her and put the packsaddle on. One flipped the cinch under her belly and when the other caught the ring, he put the latigo through it and started to cinch up. Hash tried to rear and buck, but was held down by George and his strong obedient horse. The cinch was tightened, fastened, and a heavy box placed on either side simultaneously so the saddle would not slip, and, with Hash trembling and attempting to plunge at every movement of the men, fastened firmly in place with the final hitch. George gave the animal a foot or so more freedom on her lead rope, led her in a circle and brought her back.

"She's packed," he said. "Let's get on the trail."

There were 21 horses in our pack train that day, 16 of Riviere's and five of ours. George, of course, took the lead with frequently rebellious Hash only a few feet behind. Ruth and I, with our other horses, brought up the rear. Many times, as the trail wound through the trees or twisted through rough terrain, we saw only a horse or two in front of us, and there were frequent intervals when we didn't see George for 15 or 20 minutes. The pace was brisk and any loitering meant trotting to catch up. When a pack developed trouble the rest of the train wound on like a giant disjointed serpent with no stopping, while several men repacked.

We swept northward up the valley of the North Saskatchewan, crossing and recrossing the stream, now so close to its source that it posed no threat. Then we left the river bottom and made the long hard climb on ladder-like switchbacks up the two- or three-thousand-foot "big hill." Through the trees one occasionally caught glimpses of the Saskatchewan Glacier stretching westward and upward between the two flanking ice-crested giants, Mount Saskatchewan, 10,964 feet high and Mount Athabasca, 11,452 feet.

Late that afternoon we stopped at Camp Parker at the junction of two trails, the main one through Sunwapta Pass, 6,675 feet, and the other through Nigel Pass, 7,298 feet. Both passes led to the Arctic watershed.

"Sure feels like the Arctic," George shivered the next morning. "Here you don't have to chew. You just let your teeth chatter."

Camp Parker — and I never did find the significance of the name — was a long-established campsite. A school exercise book fastened by a string to the wall inside the log cabin acted as a guest registrar, with names from all around the world and with dates over the last three decades. The trees around the cabin bore many initials and names and several skilfully carved tributes to Teacher's Highland

Nigel Pass, 7,298 feet high, leads to the Arctic watershed. "Here, you don't have to chew. You just let your teeth chatter," according to George. Cliff and Ruth and the Rivieres stop over here for a day at Camp Parker.

Cream. There were three parties there before ours made the fourth: one in the cabin, one in a teepee and one in tents.

We stopped over for a day here, socializing, helping the other three parties pack and get away, and when we had the top of the pass entirely to ourselves, we shod the horses and did other camp chores. We also loafed.

Over a noon lunch George offered to trade us a horse for Hash.

"She'll never make a good pack animal," he said. "She's hound-gutted. And she's got the idea she can get away with anything so she won't be reliable for a long time to come. I'll give you an animal that isn't as much horse, but one you'll be able to use every day. You really need another horse."

That afternoon he put the lead rope of a little brown gelding with a rough coat and a droll expression of determination in my hand.

"Here's the horse," he said. "Try him."

I did, and the ride was as smooth as proverbial silk.

"Your horses are all big-barrelled," he said. "Any of them spread a small person like Ruth too far apart and make her tired" ... Ruth had indeed suffered from fatigue ... "so a small horse, easier to mount, would be just the thing."

Ruth took a ride. "Oh, he's wonderful!" she exclaimed, and there was a look on her face such as I had seen when she spotted her mother and sister at Lake Louise.

From that moment Ruth's original mount, Rex, became our third packhorse and Cougar, the new one, became hers and was renamed Peanuts.

Peanuts, small, smooth-gaited and knowledgeable, had been taught as a packhorse to avoid hitting trees with his burdens, and he brought a new level of enjoyment and a new love into Ruth's life.

Hash also found her place. George, having decided she would never make a good packhorse, wondered aloud if she could buck him off. Catching her in, he saddled and stepped aboard, only to be jolted across the opening in a head-down, stiff-legged, grunting buck that shook the glen. But he stayed on top, pulled her head up and trotted her back, patting her on the neck and grinning.

"And now she's been rid," he said. "She's sure strong. I think I'll make her lead saddle horse in this outfit."

And he did. Hash carried her name and her rider out onto the trail and took as an excuse anything, such as a fluttering leaf, to try and dump him, but at the end of the day, George sang her praises.

"She's the best," he said. "She can buck as hard in the evening as she can in the morning. She's my Gypsy Sweetheart. And if I call her sweetheart, all the women within hearing distance will think I'm talking to them, so I'll do just that."

Peanuts, a true packhorse, brings a new level of enjoyment to Ruth after George gives him to her in exchange for the rebellious Hash.

And all the while we were with them, Gypsy led the pack train, and never failed to prance into camp at the end of the day.

We left Camp Parker through Nigel Pass and got onto the headwaters of the Brazeau River, travelling for an easy few hours at right angles to the main trail from Lake Louise to Jasper. George had been told that this trail, although a little longer, was easier, missed the Sunwapta Canyon and had better horse feed. That evening, unknowingly camped within a quarter of a mile of the warden's cabin on the Brazeau, George declared he smelled unfamiliar smoke and went along the trail to investigate.

In an hour he returned, obviously quite pleased with his walk. Smiling from ear to ear, he introduced the park ranger, Charlie Matheson, his wife Mona, and their 10-year-old guest, Ralph Wells.

"They are going to Jasper, starting in the morning," George said, "so we might as well go with them."

Next morning when the dust of departure had settled and each loose horse had found its place in the train, we were 27 horses strong, strung out over almost a quarter of a mile of trail.

It was a long day, but an easy one, through big timbers, past the azure waters of Brazeau Lake, up a narrow valley and over Poboktan Pass. The day before, trail singing had been instituted with George, Ruth and Ralph soloing, and the whole entourage frequently joining in. The horses seemed to swing in unison, the hours and the miles slipped pleasantly by, and we arrived at the "waterfall" cabin of the Mathesons on the Poboktan River, 18 miles from their other one on the Brazeau.

Here a pall of smoke was seen in the west, and the ranger reported, after a phone call to Jasper, that there was a fire on the B.C. side of the Tonquin Valley, and another near Red Pass junction on the CNR. Here also a group of three men got into a fierce argument about whether one could get through the country west of Tonquin, one declaring it was utterly impossible. The ranger, Matheson, didn't know. It was B.C. territory, and beyond park jurisdiction or study. It was here also that six big trout mysteriously appeared at the "cook-tent." There were no explanations.

Next day we swept smoothly down to the Sunwapta River and the "home" cabin of the Mathesons, a short distance below the confluence of the Poboktan. Here we stayed for a day to rest the horses, then for three days to wait out a rainstorm. During these four days we washed and repaired clothes, patched gear and read maps. Map reading was more profitable than book reading. Maps with their contour lines, lakes and rivers told us that if we had come from Camp Parker over Sunwapta Pass, we would have followed the infant Sunwapta River down through a heavy canyon to its union with the muddy Athabasca. On the other side of this river, streams flowed in from the Columbia Icefield and from places with such intriguing names as Chaba Icefield, Fortress Lake, Listening Mountain. Picture-conjuring place names they were, but they and

A tree stump serves as a handy mirror-holder as Cliff shaves, using the frayed end of a packing rope to create a lather.

the trails to some of them had to be reluctantly folded away with the maps, because they were not for us. They were on the other side of the river ... and we were heading for Jasper.

One day, when the rain had slowed down to a drizzle, horses' feet were inspected and shoes, where necessary, were applied. Gypsy, alias Hash, fiercely resisted having her hind feet shod, dancing on three while her fourth foot was tied to her tail and the shoe nailed on.

"Now she's shod north, south, east and west," said George.

There were mornings of waking up to hear the water plop on the tent a few feet from our nose, to listen intently to hear if anyone was stirring, and, reassured, go contentedly back to sleep again.

There were evenings, in the hospitable trail home of the Mathesons, with songs and homey games, talking and planning for the future. Everybody, it seemed, had dreams of a dude ranch with a beautiful fireplace in a beautiful cabin beside a beautiful lake ... and the locale extended from the foothills of Alberta to the goldfields of British Columbia.

On the fifth day all changed. The weather had cleared, horses were packed and in a few miles we met the road crew that was building the highway out from the Jasper end toward Lake Louise. Here the Mathesons exchanged their horses for a small truck, crossed the Athabasca River on the new highway bridge and went on their way toward Jasper, while the rest of us took the horse trail down the east side of the river. West of us arose the tremendous peak of Mount Edith Cavell, 11,033 feet, a memorial to the martyred nurse who died in front of a German firing squad in October of 1915. She had been matron of a Belgian Red Cross hospital in Brussels and was a member of a group helping some 200 Allied soldiers to rejoin their armies. The Germans regarded this

Athabasca Falls is close to the spot where traders bound for the territory beyond the Rockies would begin the grand traverse to the Columbia River.

as treason. Sir Richard McBride, premier of British Columbia, proposed that the highest peak in the Canadian Rockies, Mount Robson, be named in her honour. Other peaks in the Rockies were suggested as well as some in Quebec. Prime Minister Sir Robert Borden asked the Geographic Board of Canada to deal with the proposal.

This board chose the peak that had been a guide to early explorers, the mountain marking the entrance to Athabasca Pass, the one the voyageurs called La Montagne de la Grande Traverse. At the foot of it the Whirlpool River flowing out from Athabasca Pass joins the Athabasca River. Here the trade goods and the human personnel bound for the territory beyond the Rockies began the grand traverse to the Columbia River. It was named Edith Cavell in March 1916.

Much of the time horses were used in the portage. In the winter dogs were frequently the motive power, and when these failed the voyageur himself packed the loads.

It was natural that at this point, where canoes were exchanged for horses and vice versa, a herd of pack animals should be retained, and it was through the pastures of these vanished pack ponies that we rode. It had been called Buffalo Prairies, but the buffalo had all been killed by the 1870s, and, when the railway trains had replaced the pack trains, the horses also disappeared.

At the north end we dropped through the Devil's Gateway down the steep pitch of trail by Old Fort Point, clattered across the Athabasca on a sturdy bridge and were in the village of Jasper.

Someone had told George a good place to camp was near the racetrack southwest of town. There was fine grazing there for the horses and a good tent site along the Miette River, about a half-mile from town.

It had only one problem: there were too many bears.

We were not aware when we set up camp that less than a hundred yards away, across the pool-like Miette River, was the community garbage dump, a magnet for bears — and that they could swim the stream as easily as they could cross it on the nearby bridge.

Scarcely had we sat down to supper an hour after our arrival, and the tents not yet all set up, when a small black bear was seen rooting among a pile of camp effects with the obvious intention of helping himself to anything edible. Bob, the extremely useful police dog travelling with the Rivieres, gave voice and the little bear went up a big tree and sat on a limb about 50 feet from the ground and out of reach of the watchful Bob.

"We've got to teach this fellow that he can't visit without an invitation," George declared, "and then send him back as a messenger to his friends."

Accordingly, all evening when the bear showed signs of coming to the ground, a rock chucked against the tree trunk changed his mind. The last we saw of him in the dusk showed that he had worn all the hair off his rear where he had sat on the limb. He was gone in the morning and Bob, the dog, wore an embarrassed look, because he had obviously gone to sleep in the night.

We hadn't impressed the lesson on the bear, however, for on the second morning, Ruth and I were disturbed by the sound of our saddles being knocked over just outside the tent, followed almost immediately by ripping canvas as a hairy arm reached through the opening.

We heard someone cry, "There's a bear outside the Kopas tent!"

We were glad it wasn't already inside, glad also to hear Bob's bark, and to see the bear depart after an exchange of insults.

The bear went up a tree, a 25-foot spruce, the dog holding him there. We joined the Rivieres at their breakfast table, and while we ate, George sized up the situation.

"We've got to teach them a lesson," he said.

Then suddenly he jumped to his feet.

"Let's rope him!" he said, and striding to his saddle, took a lariat and went over to the spruce.

But the bear didn't like the idea. As we approached he wiggled to the far side of the tree; and as George cast the loop up at him, he kept the trunk and some of the branches between his head and the flying loop.

A dozen times were enough to prove that cowboy tactics were useless. Dropping the rope, George, assisted by Ray and Slim, grabbed the six-inch tree trunk and started to shake it. Their first attempts were not very successful and brought the bear down only a few feet before he recovered his grip on the tree and climbed up again. Then, in unison, the three men brought the tree as far over as they could, and let it snap back, and the bear was wrenched from its perch.

Snarling and spitting, it crashed through the limbs of the tree and tumbled to the ground.

In the split second that the bear lay there winded, Slim leaped on the animal as if it had been a steer in a stampede corral, seized a fistful of hair and hide underneath each of its ears and with elbows close in on the animal's shoulders and his feet drawn up and knees clamped into the barrel, was prepared to ride it.

Again the bear had different ideas. Frightened and angry, it attempted to rid itself of its rider. For several seconds all we could see was a rolling, roaring bundle of blue jeans and black bear, twigs and earth tossed around, and a dog barking hysterically.

Suddenly the bundle broke, the bear bounded for the river, pursued by the dog to the water's edge, and Slim picked himself up from the ground.

His crazy adventure had cost him a badly torn shirt and a scratch across the back of his right hand.

We suffered no more from bears in Jasper.

Jasper, like Banff, is the product of a railway and a richly endowed natural environment, each park area being created only a few years after the advent of the railway, and each town commenced with the creation of the parks. Banff is about three decades older than Jasper, yet Jasper's history outdates that of Banff. David Thompson trod its site in his 1810 approach to Athabasca Pass, and from that date until the abandonment of the overland routes to the Pacific Ocean, Jasper, on one site or other, even under different names, served the travelling public and the fur-trading business. In the 1860s, Cariboo-bound gold-seekers pastured their stock there before the push through Yellowhead Pass, and in the 1870s, hopes were entertained that the Canadian Pacific Railway would go through there. Sandford Fleming strongly recommended this route through Yellowhead for the railway.

Then in 1905, not one but two railways went through Jasper, the Grand Trunk Pacific and the Canadian Northern. Jasper Park was created in 1907. The two railways were shortly taken over by the federal government and became part of the Canadian National Railways, and during the Second World War, 250 miles or so of duplicating trackage were removed to provide steel for the war effort.

When we rode into Jasper that evening of August 2, 1933, it was a quiet little town at the end of a highway from the prairies, beginning to stir with expectation of getting its highway link to Banff. Yet packhorses were almost less of a novelty than cars, and our advent created no particular interest.

We learned that the only trail leading westward was along the Miette River to Yellowhead Pass and down the Fraser River. At Goat River, an old mining trail led to Barkerville.

"Barkerville's only 60 miles from Quesnel," George said. "I sure wish you would throw your lot in with us."

It would have been better for us if we had, but when the Riviere party left on the third morning, we were not part of it.

Nearing Jasper, we kept hearing of the wonders of the Tonquin Valley to the southwest. We wanted to see it and maybe use it as a jumping-off place for our attempt to go through to the goldfields on a trail of our own devising.

All those to whom we suggested the idea in Jasper were alike in condemning the project. It was a wild country. No one had ever gone through it. Yes, surely, you could take the old Athabasca Trail up the Whirlpool, but that would carry you, if you got through, to the Columbia, nowhere near the goldfields or Quesnel. The Rivieres had had their troubles there. Crazy to try it! Taylor, the photographer in Jasper, offered his hospitality, friendship and advice: "If there was a trail, you'd need six weeks. Since there isn't one, you'll need six months. And in six months nothing will be moving but snow owls and blizzards." Ranger Charlie Matheson had said, "Never take an outfit down a mountain you can't get back up." And someone else, whose name I didn't record, told us that even to consider it, we were "crazier than coots at the full of the moon."

We listened, but not enough, for when we put heavy packs on the horses and left Jasper a day after the Rivieres and headed for the Tonquin, we had not fully cancelled the idea of trying to beat our way through to the mining area.

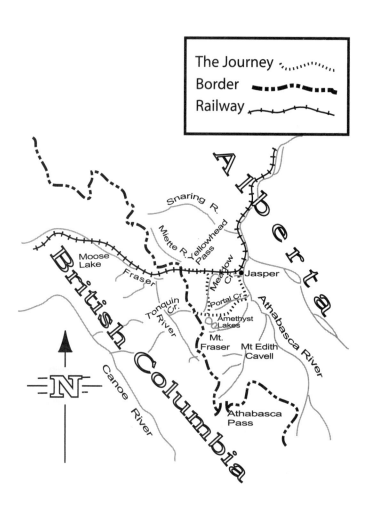

The Journey ⋅⋅⋅⋅⋅⋅⋅⋅⋅⋅⋅
Border ━⋅━⋅━⋅━
Railway ╁╁╁╁╁╁╁

Snaring R.

Alberta

Miette R. Yellowhead Pass

Moose Lake

Fraser

Meadow Cr.

Jasper

Portal Cr.

Tonquin River

Amethyst Lakes

Mt. Fraser

Mt Edith Cavell

Athabasca River

British Columbia

N

Canoe River

Athabasca Pass

The Tonquin Adventure

Tonquin! Many people in Jasper stated that it was the ultimate in mountain beauty, a valley perched high in the mountains to the southwest of them between Athabasca Pass and Yellowhead Pass. The Mathesons had told us about Tonquin, had said that "up there" were huge quartz crystals. Somebody else said that Tonquin was the ultimate in mud and flies.

"You haven't seen anything until you've been to the Tonquin," they said.

Tonquin! The name itself is an echo from the fur trade, like so many others that geographers have applied to the area, or that have been retained. From those dramatic times came the names for the major passes, the Athabasca and the Yellowhead and of other features such as the Astoria River, Simon Peak and Mount Fraser, even the Fraser River itself, which is born in the district.

Maybe it was the gentlemen of the Interprovincial Boundary Commission who worked along the Alberta–British Columbia boundary from 1913 to 1924 who were responsible for such imaginative names as Lectern Peak, The Forum, and Rostrum Hill, all features around the Tonquin Valley. It might have been they who applied to the row of rocky summits that bound the valley on the west the picturesque medieval names of Portcullis, Dungeon, Drawbridge, Bastion, Turret, Postern and Moat.

Tonquin! That was the name of the ship in which the Astorians came to a violent end off Vancouver Island in 1811, when its irascible commander precipitated an Indian attack. The first wave of Natives was thrown back. Of the crew of 23 on the ship, only five remained alive, and one of these, (Lewis, the ship's clerk), was wounded. The morning after the attack, the ship, sails half-hoisted and hanging slack, was still in the bay and as the Indians surrounded her, Lewis appeared on deck and invited them aboard. He then disappeared below, and, when the decks were literally swarming with Natives, the ship blew up with a terrific explosion. Lewis had fired the powder magazine in retaliation for the attack. His companions had slipped away in the night, but Lewis, disabled by his wound, had elected to stay and exact his terrible revenge. The others, forced ashore by wind, were found by the Indians and died a tortured death.

Among those killed in the attack on the *Tonquin* was Alexander Mackay, the cousin and lieutenant of Alexander Mackenzie, who had accompanied him on his trip to the Pacific in 1793. Mackay had subsequently joined the Astorians and sailed on the *Tonquin*.

Tonquin! The name appeared at least four times on our maps and it haunted us for a long time after our visit there.

When we left Jasper a day after the Rivieres, we took a different direction. They went along the Miette River toward Yellowhead Pass, while we followed the beckoning wedge of Mount Edith Cavell, the mountain of the Grande Traverse. But instead of following the Athabasca to the Whirlpool and then up to Athabasca Pass, we took the trail up Portal Creek and on the second afternoon looked from the high Maccarib Pass into the Tonquin Valley.

Tonquin! From the gentle green slopes in front of us, over to the Amethyst Lakes and to the top of the Ramparts, on the continental ridgepole, it was an amazing view. One looked at it first as one great canvas, then picked out sections for more intimate study. First the Ramparts, a row of huge pinnacles beyond the lakes, rising three and four thousand feet above the valley floor and looking as if some prehistoric monster had leaped from behind nearby mountains, humped its back, swung its huge tail back and forth to scoop out valleys, then, with back arched and head down, had turned to stone. The rubble of rock around its base, enough to make a respectable ridge elsewhere, here looked only like the skin pushed aside as the bones protruded. There was no doubt we were looking into the Tonquin Valley, and no doubt that the Ramparts — Paragon, Dungeon, Redoubt, Drawbridge, Bastion, Turret, Mount Geikie and Barbican Peak — constituted one of the most amazing, spectacular and savagely beautiful of all the component ranges of the Rockies.

Through an obvious portal to the northwest, Tonquin Pass introduced the Pacific watershed and British Columbia, from here a sea of mountains each as faceless as individuals in a crowd.

Just south and west of the Ramparts a mad tangle of great peaks broadened the backbone of the continent, creating a background for the Ramparts and, providing a birthplace for the infant Fraser, British Columbia's longest and most important solely owned river.

The actual source is in the Fraser Pass, 6,500 feet high, not more than 15 miles from the Athabasca Pass. From here the little stream prattles northwest, gaining in volume and velocity on every mountain and in every valley that it passes through. By the time it reaches Tête Jaune Cache it is big enough to be riotous and dangerous or to carry a load. Following the Rocky Mountain Trench it makes frequent loops but follows in general a remarkably straight valley northwestward for nearly 200 miles, to turn south near Prince George. Searching for a way to the sea it flows the length of the southern half of the province to rush furiously through the canyons of the Coast Range. Emerging from these it slides quietly for a few miles and joins the sea just north of the 49th parallel of latitude, almost a thousand miles from its source.

In front of us now the Tonquin smiled, blue and green and white under brilliant sunshine and a flawless sky. As we sat and absorbed this astonishing panorama, a little cabin, a toy structure set upon a knoll near the stream that clattered down from the pass, drew our attention. It was the final factor in the complete beauty of the picture. The trail led toward it, and the horses, sensing freedom from their burdens, followed it willingly.

On closer approach, however, the cabin had a less attractive appearance. The windows were all stoutly laced and meshed with barbed wire, and the door similarly reinforced. At one time there had been a decking on the porch. Now there were only a few boards in front of the door. The place looked like either a prison for holding people in, or a fort for holding people out.

In this case the wire was intended to keep out grizzly bears. A few years ago the warden, Goodair, returned one afternoon to find that a bear had come in at one window, smashed everything in the cabin, and left through the window on the other side. A week or so later Goodair was coming up the hill to get his horses. With his head down and his mind on the job, he did not notice that he had walked between a grizzly and her cubs. The mother bear immediately launched a savage attack, and was not satisfied until she had killed Goodair and mutilated his body. His grave is a few yards from the cabin.

There was no response to our knock.

We had been told in Jasper that in Tonquin, we would meet the ultimate in mountain beauty, flies and mud. Half an hour before reaching the warden's cabin we conceded the first, and half an hour later we were painfully ready to grant the accuracy of the other two. We had also been told that the nicest place to camp was across the valley, where one could look into that magnificent mass of major peaks south of the Ramparts. Less than a quarter-mile from the warden's cabin, the trail became just a black pathway through peaty, cinch-deep mud, one that divided to lead through more mud to other parts of the country. At the same time we were attacked by horseflies that bit and buzzed and nearly drove us and the animals crazy, until, in the cool of evening, they withdrew.

The campsite, when we did find it, was indeed a beauty. From the top of a firm little flat about 50 feet above the valley floor, with a few trees and no undergrowth, we looked out upon the Amethyst

The Ramparts, rising above the pristine Amethyst Lakes, look as though a prehistoric monster had leapt from behind nearby mountains, swung its huge tail around to scoop out valleys, then, with back arched and head down, turned to stone.

Lakes reaching down a corridor between high mountains feeding rivers of ice into their own reflections. Framed by the spruce of our camp, the view was a rare gem.

For the first time on the trip, our horses wanted to be in camp so much that they were almost a nuisance. The flies, which merely bothered us, drove the horses nearly frantic. We built one smudge, then two, and the horses got some relief, particularly when they straddled the fires. Toward evening the horseflies ceased but then the mosquitoes arrived.

In the evening the warden, John Curren, came over. A true mountain man, he had been born in the Rockies in 1887 and had spent his entire life packing, guiding, trapping and in park service. Like most of his kind, he enjoyed a visit, but he also felt it his duty to know what was happening in his area, and who was travelling therein. He had been a ranger in the Kananaskis country before the war, had built the Mud Lake Trail and the cabin there, and had built a bridge across the Smith–Dorrien.

He told us of the Goodair tragedy, and felt that the bear, having killed a human once, was extremely dangerous.

Two or three years ago the Amethyst Lakes had been stocked with 50,000 trout fingerlings for the pleasure of future anglers.

"Just look at the little stinkers now, would you," he said, pointing to the nearest lake, where, in the last of the sunlight it looked as if the water was being flailed with hailstones.

No, he had never heard of a trail down the Tonquin Creek. He had been here for two years, but since it was beyond park boundaries he had no reason to go there. Yes, there could be a trail, also, maybe not.

Next morning dawned crystal clear and, leaving three of the horses hobbled, we saddled the other two and by seven o'clock were working across the mud at the end of the lake with the intention of climbing the shoulder of Mount Clitheroe from where, Curren had told us, we could get a commanding view of the country.

Before long we were above timberline. Tonquin lay at our feet, and the Ramparts across the way held up their beauty for inspection in the early morning sun. Away to the south, glaciers gleamed and shone among the peaks, while to the north, the open door of Tonquin Pass permitted a view of the frozen wave crests of the sea of mountains in British Columbia. Beneath us lay the shimmering expanses of the twin Amethyst Lakes, reflecting peak and glacier except when a light breeze played on the surface and turned it to liquid silver. On a patch of snow a quarter of a mile away a caribou loafed, having come up to avoid the flies, and nearby a little wren bobbed on rocks and the tonic perfume of pine and spruce filled the air.

It was in these conditions of lyric loveliness that we decided we would venture into Tonquin Pass, though it was low and scarcely recognizable. One of our maps gave the summit of the pass as 6,390 feet, only 10 feet higher than Moat Lake at 6,380 feet, yet 60 feet lower than Amethyst Lakes, at 6,450 feet, which drain out through the Astoria River. Moat Lake was a little spot of blue at the top of the pass, reflecting the adjoining beauties of the Alberta and British Columbia scenery, while a meadow stretched out of Alberta down the shallow valley into the other watershed as far as we could see. Beyond that rose a sea of mountains with

76

Glaciers gleaming among the peaks hold up their beauty for inspection in the early-morning sun. Ruth and Cliff leave from this point to tackle the Tonquin Valley, a pass that proves to be an incredible challenge to the honeymooners.

no end, massed and tangled together, looking purple and white in the distance.

The Tonquin, flowing out of the pass at 6,390 feet, joins the Fraser River in about 12 miles, and in another 12 miles or so, where it narrowly avoids Yellowhead Lake, it has dropped to 3,600 feet, indicating abrupt descents.

The morning of our departure from Amethyst Lakes was sparkling and fly-free, insects having been numbed by a sharp frost. By 8:45, using a "Riviere rope corral" to capture our horses, we were ready for the trail. Directly north of our camp a path took us into a jungle of timberline vegetation, where it lost itself and left us pushing our way in the general direction of Moat Lake. We moved over what in ages past had been a moraine pushed into place by a huge ice floe that had scooped the bed for the Amethyst Lakes, pushed its load of boulders over what is now the pass, and, retreating, left lakes with grinding icebergs which had levelled the rocks into a semblance of massive cobblestones. Another glacial thrust had pushed a ridge into place, permitting the waters of the now-called

Amethyst Lakes to flow eastward and northward to the Arctic instead of the Pacific, as they once undoubtedly had done. The cracks between these immense cobbles, and in fact most of the cobbles themselves, had become covered with mud and grass, forcing us into very slow going.

Mud persisted as far as Moat Lake, and at the far end of this we found the remains of a large four- or five-year-old camp. Across little dimpling Moat Lake rose the rugged Ramparts. All about were the wide meadows of the pass, and a chill breeze from the west promised freedom from insects.

For a few miles we rode down a pleasant vale, gradually working into timber, enjoying it immensely, not knowing we were heading into trouble. The timber thickened, and a spruce swamp forced a detour. Small but deeply cut stream beds lay across our path, necessitating searches for spots where we could get into and out of them. We tried following close by Tonquin Creek. Once, a tree too big for our camp axes forced our horses to drop from the main bank onto a narrow ledge just above the stream, then turn sharply round the broken butt of the log and make a difficult scramble back onto the bank.

Lower down, we walked the horses over huge boulders where one moment of imbalance would have thrown them into the water. We decided to leave the stream and went higher on the hill, but found the brush too thick and came down again. We navigated a stretch of slide boulders covered with moss and brush, giving the horses cruel work as they fell and struggled, pulled and sweated. We rose higher on the hill. The stream vanished into a canyon.

We moved with fair speed for a quarter of a mile until we came to a solid bank of timber on a slope too steep for horses. A few yards back, a slope of rock offered a slide down to what appeared to be an alternative route. My horse, Dick, slid down on his haunches, front feet braced. Dream followed, O'Hara picked his way down by inches. Ruth followed safely until Rex, in the rear, fell and stumbled into them. A young pine tree got in the way of the falling trio and just stopped them. Rex walked away; Peanuts, with Ruth still in the saddle, got on his feet again.

We stopped for a few moments. Ruth appeared unshaken by her close call. Rex's pack had to be rearranged.

We could see the valley of the Fraser ahead of us, not more than a mile across. On the far side the sun was picking out individual trees.

We struggled down an inch at a time, then suddenly realized the sun had set. Going down another incline, then a few rods above a narrow ledge and up against a blockade of fallen timber, we realized it would take us an hour to move another 50 yards. Above us rose a steep bank. Below, the shelf dropped for a frightening distance too nearly perpendicular to be looked at twice.

So we camped there, tying the dispirited horses to trees, and by the time we had our meal, it was dark. There was no room for a tent, so packing boxes were placed at our feet to prevent us from sliding out of our blankets in the night. Below us Tonquin Creek roared while above us trees rose to the star-studded sky.

Once during the night I woke, and in turning over, woke Ruth.

"Isn't the moon grand?" she said, and I noticed for the first time the silvery disc pushing beams of light through the trees. A horse sighed in its sleep. Things might have been much worse: it could have been raining or snowing.

Next morning, while Ruth prepared breakfast, I attacked the timber ahead, cut for an hour or so, then took a short walk to see what we were coming into, and went back to camp. When we had eaten, Ruth came down to look for the trail with me.

Below the spot where I had ceased chopping, we worked through a tangle of fallen timber thick enough to deter a mountain lion. The hill became so steep we had to let ourselves down hand under hand. On our left the stream leaped down a bed of boulders and raced into a shallow canyon.

We were stuck. We realized at last why there were no game trails on the mountainside. Game does not travel where it is unprofitable. A blaze here and there on trees could have been the work of a trapper — we had seen his spring steel traps hanging on trees in several places, and had taken them as an indication we were travelling in the right direction. Several times we had seen trees that had been cut to allow broad packs. But in every case the trails had petered out. The trapper had gone elsewhere, the other parties had gone back.

So must we.

"Do you think the horses can get back up to where Rex nearly knocked Peanuts and me down?" Ruth asked.

I didn't know. It was a worrisome thought.

Our troubles started almost immediately. In negotiating a climb which made the horses claw for footing, O'Hara, always skeptical about the party's leadership, attempted a route of his own, overbalanced when his pack hit a tree and rolled over twice before he found his feet again. In his pack were a portable typewriter and a mirror, which we assumed were broken. But with his pack well bound with canvas and outwardly intact, we didn't investigate.

Ruth decided to lead Rex, who seemed to be bumping trees too often with his pack, so fastening the reins around the cheek-strap in Peanut's bridle, she let him follow behind. After a struggle in a short detour from the trail we had followed down, we discovered that Peanuts was not with us. Ruth went back to where she had last seen him, then right back to where we had spent the night, and came back with a very worried look. We had lost the horse.

We picked up his tracks, and followed them to the site of the redoubtable rock. We had thought he might be stuck there. But his tracks showed at the top. We were relieved to know a horse could indeed get up there, but feared we had lost him.

We brought the other four horses to the foot of the rock slope, and tried to take the packhorses up. Rex fell at the first attempt, O'Hara refused to try, Dream made three valiant attempts but her pack pulled off balance each time, and Dick went up without mishap. Then we took the packs off the others, attached lash ropes to their halter shanks and fastened them to a tree up the slope, finally getting all three to the top.

It was now five o'clock, and we had horses at the top, packs at the bottom. It was too late to drag the packs up the slope, so we secured them to a tree, and grabbing a handful of dried fruit set out to find grass.

Dick's trail-following genius took us within an hour to a little grazing spot where we picketed the horses, ate our dried fruits and drank some water. Then Ruth stepped over to the edge of the glade, and found the spurs she had left looped over Peanut's saddle horn.

We knew now that Peanuts had been there, had eaten, had probably tried to roll and had dropped the spurs.

We made a bed of our saddle blankets and slept. Waking refreshed, we untangled the picket ropes of the horses and when they had eaten every blade of grass in sight, started back for our packs.

It took us two hours to haul, shove and carry three packhorse loads up the steep slope, but we eventually accomplished it, packed the horses and were on our way.

We passed our overnight bivouac, and crossed Tonquin Creek. Here Dick, whom I had come to regard as infallible in trail following, wanted to leave our downward path and follow what I thought was a moose track up a little knoll. We stopped to study the situation. Ruth thought those were not moose tracks in the moss, but horse tracks, Peanuts', in fact.

Given his head, Dick stepped out eagerly. I had further misgivings when I could not see any tracks in front of us, but Dick pushed on, ears forward in full attention. We went through some low conifers, saw a meadow ahead and some more trees, and beyond them a little brown horse wearing a saddle and a bridle, and a pleased, well-fed look about him, Peanuts!

Ruth petted him, talked affectionately to him, stepped into the saddle and rode a few steps to make sure she wasn't dreaming. Then noting that the case for field glasses, which had hung around the saddle horn, was empty, we looked around for the glasses. After a few minutes, I said, "There isn't one chance in a million that we could find them. Let's get going!"

But Ruth would not give up. "Peanuts, where are those field glasses?" she demanded.

As if in answer, Peanuts walked not towards the horses, but to a small spruce tree, and stopped. There at his feet lay the field glasses.

Next day we waded through the Tonquin mud and the voracious flies to the warden's cabin, to find it locked. We were unpacking beside it when John Curren rode up, having just come over Maccarib Pass.

"Am I glad to see you!" he exclaimed as he dismounted. "I've been to Jasper and everything I learned about the lower Tonquin was bad. I was going on a search for you in about another three days. You will be my guests in the cabin."

The Tonquin cabin that night became a centre of population. The warden had brought with him a guest from Jasper, a young man by the name of Davey Jones, questing for the famous rock crystals. Within minutes after our arrival another three rode up, asked if they could use the cabin for cooking and pitched a tent beside it.

One of these men, Rutter, a Canadian National Railways fireman, proved a very garrulous fellow, telling tales as he helped with the cooking for his party. Bears? They weren't invincible, as witness the account of one Indian hunter, Louis Shuswap, who met a big grizzly, pumped a rifle full of lead into it and then met its charge by seizing its drooling tongue and holding it out so the beast couldn't bite him. The bear died from the shock of the bullets and the man escaped with his own hide intact.

About midnight three noisy men arrived. They wanted to cook some food and stay the night. Curren grunted assent (which meant full use of the cabin), rolled over and while the men worked and talked, lay as if asleep.

We became better acquainted next morning. The leader, Captain E. R. Gibson, was from Winterburn, near Edmonton; Bob Hind was from Calgary; and the third, E. L. Woolf, an electrical engineer, was from Ardsley, New York. After they had

After a much-needed rest in the Tonquin ranger's cabin, Cliff and Ruth are once again ready to hit the pack trail.

eaten breakfast they put on their climbers' boots and went back 15 miles to Fraser Glacier to retrieve the rest of their supplies.

We rested that day. In the evening, bringing Dick to the cabin to put a shoe on him — we had lost 11 shoes out of 20 in the Tonquin — Curren gave him a feed of oats, as he was getting thin with the responsibility of leading a pack-string.

"You know," he said, as he patted Dick's neck, "these blooded horses shouldn't be taken on the long trail. They haven't got enough hide or hair to protect themselves from flies or cold. The best kinds are those cayuses you can't kill with a shotgun."

Our horses, with the exception of Peanuts, who fitted into the unkillable class, were in bad shape. Tonquin, the sternest teacher we had had on this trip, had shown us we did not have the time, strength or reserves to push through an untracked wilderness. Henceforth, every effort to conserve our resources must be made. Any further flirtations with adventure could well jeopardize our chance of winning through to Bella Coola.

We hauled out our maps and discussed the territory westward. The Rivieres had taken the Fraser River–Goat River route and it looked to be the only way westward.

"And if you think it's going to be lacking in excitement," said Rutter, the railroader, sitting in on the study, "you can blow your whistle again. You go right along the rail right-of-way right between the rails a lot of the way, and there's a place along Moose Lake, where you have the lake right below you and a high rock-cut reaching for the sky above you. No chance to get off … not a snowball's chance in a furnace. If a train catches you there, it would take a rainstorm to wash you off the rocks. Nothing has happened yet, but watch out. The law of averages will start to take over!"

The next day we dropped to the Miette River by way of the Meadow Creek Trail, a well-engineered, skilfully constructed trail that speeded us through sky-high meadows and colourful canyons. The terrain was in part similar to that which had treated us so roughly, but now it was a pleasure to travel and very soon we had reached the Miette Valley and were crossing the little river in it on a pack bridge. There was a tote road that we followed west for an hour or so before making camp beside the sleepy stream.

In camp we checked our progress. We were nine days out of Jasper and nine miles — a half day's journey — from there. Our outfit was sadder and wiser, at least in the knowledge that the ridge of the Rockies could be a rough playground.

The Miette Valley westward from Jasper affords a nearly level approach to Yellowhead Pass. Jasper's altitude is 3,472 feet and Yellowhead Summit, barely 25 miles westward, is 3,711 feet, the climb being only 239, or less than a 1 percent grade. In 1862 a party of Overlanders (the first of several) travelling to the Cariboo from Fort Garry had exchanged their Red River carts for pack animals at Edmonton. They complained bitterly of the hardships they experienced in the Miette Valley. Their diaries contained references to 20 crossings of the stream. So repeated were their complaints that a group of alpinists made a special trip to investigate, and could only surmise that the difficulties might have been fallen timber and muskeg.

Misfortunes for the Overlanders were only commencing at this point. For us, the Miette Valley, with its tote roads, bridges and level ground, was a reprieve and a relaxation.

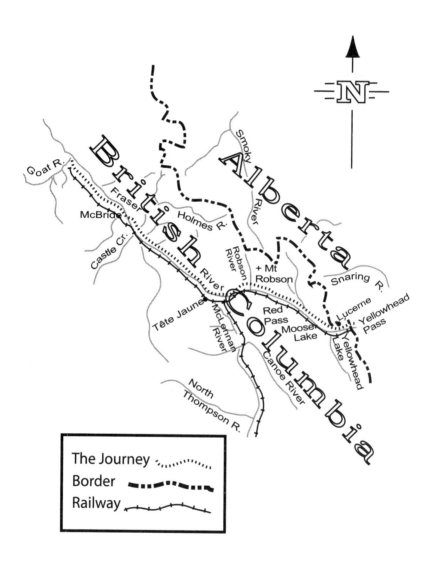

The Journey ⋯⋯⋯
Border ▬ ▬ ▬
Railway ⊬⊬⊬⊬

Yellowhead to Goat River

Yellowhead Pass was at one time an important fur trade gateway into what was then known as New Caledonia (now northern British Columbia). Brigades bound for the east ascended the Fraser as far as Tête Jaune Cache, there to meet with brigades which had come through the pass from Jasper on the Athabasca. The naming of the pass is uncertain, but is credited to the presence of a fair-haired Métis, François Decoigne, leader of a group of Indians transplanted into the area by the North West Company to collect furs.

Whether he really was a blond Métis or not, the name has appealed to geographers, for in the immediate area are Yellowhead Pass, Yellowhead Lake, Yellowhead Mountain and Yellowhead, B.C. (whistle stop), as well as Decoigne on the Alberta side, and when we had gone a few miles into B.C., there at our feet, starting bravely for the distant ocean, was an infant stream, Yellowhead Creek.

Discovering that water was flowing in the opposite direction was the traditional sign to wilderness travellers that they had crossed the watershed. We already knew, however, because a stone's throw west of where the trail left the Miette River, the summit of the pass was marked by a cairn, a warden's cabin and a bad-tempered caretaker, who, if he liked travellers, was careful to conceal it.

When the Hudson's Bay Company absorbed the North West Company in 1820, it continued to use the pass until about 1827, calling it Leather Pass because of loads of heavy leather like buffalo and moose hides that went west from the prairies to supply leather needs in New Caledonia. About that time the defile was also called Cowdung Pass or a similar name given it by the forthright voyageurs. Then, due to the development of other routes and the repeated loss of life and cargo in the rapids of the Upper Fraser, the route was abandoned and the pass forgotten, except for the occasional mountain man or trapper.

The Overlanders in 1862 had been told that the trail through the pass was a "coach road" — definitely an understatement — and in 1863, the first recorded tourists, Viscount Milton and Dr. Cheadle, came to the area, bound, like the Overlanders, for the Cariboo.

In the early part of the 20th century, two railways had come, and within a few years, one had been torn up and the steel put into the war effort. Sometimes we used the roadbed of the former railway, at others we took the tote road; often we travelled in blistering sun and were grateful for the occasional shade of tall spruce and fir trees. Our first campsite in this third entry into B.C. was at Lucerne, on Yellowhead Lake.

This had been a divisional point on the railway that had been torn up, and now the station and attendant buildings were empty, with staring windows and flapping doors. Yellowhead Lake had once been called Cowdung Lake, but recent geographers had changed the name with the same feeling they had changed Studhorse Creek to Wildhorse Creek and Gastown to Granville in Vancouver.

In Lucerne several modest little houses were occupied, one by an old trapper who congratulated us on retreating in the Tonquin.

"You're lucky you went back. Sure, there's a trail down the Fraser but she's a trap unless the water is very low, like early spring or after snappy weather in the fall. If you had got through to the Fraser you'd have been in a bad spot at this time of the year. You have to go down a canyon, and there's quicksand there. Even Rink, who knows the country, lost two horses in one trip there."

Rink, I understood, was the top outfitter of the district, and had a lake and river "just over Yellowhead Mountain" named after him.

"Did you ever have a cabin ripped open by a bear?" I asked. I had touched a sore spot indeed.

"Yes, dam' their hides. A couple of times. Just last winter one bust in ... started in through the window, thought it wasn't big enough so he just bust the wall apart, went in and tore everything to pieces. He even chewed up a suit of brand new woollen underwear."

An old suit, one with "some cooties" in it and smelling of sweat and spilled liquor, he could understand as being appealing to a bear. But to eat a new suit, "not smelly or nothing" was just plain cussedness!

Our travels were eased through this section by the tote road and frequent grassy clearings, some of them the remains of riotous camps from railway construction days, some the sad abandoned farmsteads of settlers who had been unable to cope with the wilderness and the depression. We came upon a camp of the Rivieres. We saw where the Fraser River plunged out of the mountains to join the stream flowing out of Yellowhead Lake, and we saw it become a stretch of surging rapids and then broaden out into the smiling, breeze-caressed Moose Lake.

Here, trails and tote roads converged onto the currently used railway tracks and forced equestrian travellers between the steel rails for a distance of about 10 miles. The tracks were only a few feet from the deep waters of the lake, and above the narrow cut, the mountains rose to heights of eight or nine thousand feet. While here and there it was possible to get off the rails, many of the narrow cuts afforded no such opportunity. It was because of this that Rutter, the railroader in the Tonquin Valley, had said, "if a train caught you there, it would take a rainstorm to wash you off the rocks."

We had ambled peacefully through this succession of hazards until we were within a mile or so of emerging when suddenly a premonition of danger struck us. Breaking our long-established rule of never forcing our packhorses into a trot, we hurried them briskly along the narrow cut. At the point where the mountain dropped back to permit departure from the tracks, a maintenance crew was working. The men lay down their tools as we approached.

"When is the next train due?" I asked as an opener, for there seemed a strained look about the men, as if they intended to eject us forcefully from their right-of-way.

A scream from Ruth answered my question.

"Here's a train, now!"

We had only about 10 seconds, but in that time our five horses had plunged down the embankment into a copse of trees while a passenger train went roaring by.

We talked with the foreman of the crew and watched as a second train, a freight, roared past us. In coming from the Yellowhead summit we had passed into a new time zone and our watch was an hour in error.

That night we camped at Red Pass junction, where the single railway line expands into two, one turning south at Tête Jaune Cache to follow the North Thompson, Thompson and Fraser rivers to Vancouver, the other to go along the Fraser, Nechako and Skeena rivers to Prince Rupert. For miles there were still two almost parallel scars along the mountain south of the river.

Our camp on the Robson River, another day's trip seaward, was marked by a scolding from a woman because we inadvertently rode across her hay meadow. But when our horses had another attack of homesickness and started back-trailing, her husband corralled them where they could enjoy a block of salt, and invited me to leave them there with a pile of oat hay. His name was Dennison, and he and his partner, Brittain, were guides and outfitters in the Robson area. They said they knew of an outfit that had brought a party down Tonquin Creek to the Fraser River and then out to Lucerne. All I could say was I knew an outfit that hadn't.

Mount Robson, the highest peak in the Canadian Rockies (12,972 feet), has been as reticent about the origin of its name as has Yellowhead Pass. Historians have suggested it might have been named by Yellowhead himself after his boss, Colin

Robertson of the North West Company, who, in 1820, when head of New Caledonia, turned Decoigne and his companions loose in the woods thereabouts to collect furs. Slurring of the name could account for its change. At any rate, in 1863 Milton and Cheadle refer to it without any explanation as "Robson's Peak."

That evening, heaven-high above and filling the whole northern sky, the mountain was attacked by electric storms, and, as we watched, lightning crackled and thunder vibrated to the very soles of our feet. When we thought the storms were over, we went to bed, sleeping on the tent rather than under it. When the weather was good we preferred not to erect the tent, a practice that gave us more living room and saved time.

We paid for our indulgence that night. At some stage, it was so dark that we couldn't see our watches; rain started beating down on us, and although our canvas cover kept it out from above, the volume of water falling flooded into our bed from the bottom. We lay in pitch-blackness until dawn came and we could put up a tent, erect the stove and dry our blankets. This took seven hours and we got away from that site at three in the afternoon.

Dennison had told us the tote road we were following went as far as Tête Jaune Cache — which we found, with confusing detours, to be true.

He also told us that just a few miles west there was a swift little side stream spanned by a rickety bridge. We recognized it immediately, and saw that the timbers were rotting, the decking broken and moss-covered. Underneath it a stream spewed out of the mountain carrying boulders along with it. We studied the situation, decided it was worse than a combination of the Smith–Dorrien and Spray rivers, and then carefully, prayerfully and one at a time, led the horses across without mishap.

We noted on our map that the station of Tête Jaune Cache and the whistle stop of Tête Jaune, both on the railway, were south of the river. But there were enough people on the north side to make a small wilderness community.

It was here in 1862 that the first Overlanders arrived, in a state of starvation and exhaustion, to set up camp and await others of their party. Here the group split, the larger portion electing to go down the Fraser on rafts or in canoes dug out of cottonwood trunks.

The smaller party, 36-strong and including the only woman, Mrs. Schubert, crossed the Fraser and commenced hacking their way through the jungle, first toward the Cariboo and then toward Kamloops, at whose location they could only vaguely guess. Finding progress slow along the banks of the North Thompson River, they killed their cattle, turned their horses loose and built rafts to take them downstream. At one stage they had to abandon some of the first rafts and rebuild others. One man was drowned. Some walked the last 50 miles. One of the rafts arrived in Kamloops only hours before Mrs. Schubert, who already had three children, gave birth to a fourth, a girl to whom was given the name Rose.

The larger group also had their troubles. One man died and another was drowned, but the rest of the party reached Quesnel.

Tête Jaune Cache was so named because that almost-mythical blond trader-trapper, Tête Jaune, established a cache or storage place there for his furs. It was a good choice, for it was the meeting place of the Fraser and North Thompson valleys along which trade and travel moved, and there was an abundance of open meadows for pasturing stock.

An amazing thing happened to Tête Jaune Cache in 1912. Perched near the continental divide 53 miles from Yellowhead Pass, and surrounded by the highest mountains of two ranges, it became of all things a shipbuilding centre. The Grand Trunk Pacific Railway, headed for the western ocean, had reached Mile 49. The contractors, with plans to use the Fraser River to carry construction material, bought two sternwheeler steamers that had been used on the Skeena, dismantled and packed them into 10 freight cars it and sent them to the end of steel at Mile 49. With horses, mules and steam donkeys, the ship components were dragged over the same tote road we had used to get to Tête

The Upper Fraser wends its way east of Tête Jaune Cache. In 1912, Tête Jaune Cache was the incongruous site of a shipbuilding centre.

Jaune Cache. Here, under the drip of the glaciers that crowned the continental summit, shipyards were created and the two ships, each 141.7 feet long and 34.8 feet in the beam, were rebuilt and launched.

For three years, they and other ships that joined this inland fleet plied every summer regularly between Tête Jaune Cache and Prince George, 315 miles one way by river, 180 miles by rail, and back again. Tête Jaune was the transshipping centre, warehousing and dispatching tremendous tonnages of materials that had been brought there by the newly built railway. In addition to a full load of passengers, each ship carried 300 tons of supplies per trip and pushed a scow with another 100 tons.

Even more remarkable was the appearance of a battalion of scowmen, a Legion of the Damned, who manned scows put into the water at Tête Jaune Cache with 20 or 30 tons aboard to float them downriver to the construction camps, or even to Prince George. These men, five or six to a crew, guided the rafts with sweeps, challenged the rapids that had drowned the Overlanders and defeated the voyageurs, and in four or five days, delivered their cargo to Prince George. The scows were dismantled for their lumber and the crew, returning upstream on the next steamer, would bring a freshly built one down.

Tragedies were frequent. The scowmen were devil-may-care, fatalistic and daring. Loss of scows and cargo was about 10 percent of what was loaded upriver, and about the same percentage of scowmen. In 1913 there were 1,500 scowmen on the river and in one day alone the construction company released 100 rafts carrying $250,000 in merchandise. But the days of the steamboats were numbered. They could not compete with the trains, nor go under low-level bridges, and for many months of the year they could not be used at all. So when the first train went through Prince George on January 27, 1914, that was the end of the steamboats.

Tête Jaune Cache had lost any vestige of a railway town, a river port or even a cache when we rode into it, and we had difficulty finding our way out again. There were a few houses, some occupied and some not, and many roads or trails through the new growth of cottonwood had to be explored until we found the one leading to McBride. We had been told there was a road from Tête Jaune Cache to McBride suitable for cars. We eventually found it.

One of the towns that survived the "bust" after the railroad boom, one of the very few that did not sink back again into the good black earth, was the town of McBride, now our immediate destination. For the first time on the trip we rode through good farmland with stocks of grain and cattle in the fields. The bushes alongside the road were heavy with berries and we stopped frequently to visit with the carloads of people who were picking them. From these people we learned that the good land around was offered, sometimes with improvements, at only a dollar per acre. Even at that price it did not sell, since no one had money either to buy land or start farming. Practically everyone was living on government relief. The good berry crop was a blessing, not only for immediate consumption but also for next winter.

We met the forest warden from McBride. He stopped his truck and asked our destination, route and where we had come from. We supposed it was partly a professional gesture because this was a forested country and it was his job to look after it. It also seemed that people here, as in most frontier areas, welcomed someone new to talk to.

He told us we were the third party to attempt the Goat River trail, which until this year hadn't been used for at least 20 years except by "goats, grizzlies and an occasional prospector."

"Must be a gold rush going on in the Cariboo again," he said.

Actually there was, but we didn't think we were part of it.

"Did the other parties make it through?" we asked.

"Couldn't rightly say," he countered. "Leastwise no one has gone looking for them."

One party that he was talking about, it turned out, was the Rivieres. A second party consisting of two men had stopped before reaching the Goat River. One of them had broken a leg in a stream crossing and was now in the Prince George hospital.

"It's just as well," our informant opined. "Goat River might have dealt him a worse blow than that."

At this point we told him of a fire burning against a log several miles back and he left hurriedly. We thought it was a settler's fire aimed to clear land, and that it was a shame to burn the beautiful cedars just to get them out of the way.

We came to a stout three-span bridge across the Fraser from which we could see, about a mile distant, the town of McBride. Underneath the bridge the river flowed strongly and I was glad we didn't have to swim it. Our map showed there was a ferry here but no bridge. If the ferry had still been there and on a charge basis we could have been in trouble for we had now only 10 cents between us.

Just across the bridge we met a man driving a well-fed team in a light wagon, and he stopped when we were opposite him.

"Yep," he said, after he had asked our destination, our origin and what we thought of the country, and we had expressed gratitude for the bridge. "We've had her since 1925. Before that we had a ferry, a decking on a couple of hulls and operated by the current. It was big enough to carry a team and wagon but every spring and fall there was a time when the ice stopped us. And in the winter we had to cross on the ice."

He shot a charge of tobacco juice at a rock on the edge of the road, and moved it an inch.

"Too bad, too," he continued. "It shut up a good woman." He stopped to let us register surprise. "When you came to the river and wanted the ferry, a lady named Ethel Munroe — she had a voice that carried like a hog caller's — she called the ferryman. Across town, you can see it's about a mile, the policeman would hear the call and would hunt up the ferryman and bring him to the river. I kinda miss it."

In McBride, a village of about 300 people and obviously laid out with more planning than a great many frontier towns, we tried to find someone who could tell us about the onward trail, particularly the Goat River sector. We learned that the town was named after Sir Richard McBride, premier of B.C. at the time of the town's founding, and that McBride was the "handsomest dam' premier" the province ever had. We were also told that about two weeks before, when the Rivieres' outfit had gone through, the townspeople had thrown a dance and party for them just because it was nice to see somebody new in the community. "And it was a good party. When it started to run dry the liquor vendor — he's also the postmaster and the mayor — went with the boys and got another load. Now, that was a party!"

We had almost despaired of finding anyone who could give us trail information when around a corner came a genial middle-aged Chinese man who hailed us immediately.

"Hello, people," he called. "You going someplace?"

We told him we wanted to get through to Barkerville, then to Quesnel.

"Then you want to go up the Goat River trail," he declared. "You go out of the town on that road, and after a while you go on the railway tracks — everybody does — it's the only trail. Not many trains go through here. You have to go through a railway tunnel. It's about 18 miles west of here."

He stopped and grinned at us.

"You can't miss it. It's the only way through the country. Just make sure a train is not due when you want to go through. If you do get caught by a train in there you won't freeze next winter."

"Seven or eight miles past the tunnel you come to Goat Creek. There is a good trail up the creek — for a few miles. Then, if you do not swear and use bad language, you will not be able to talk about the trail. Have you come far?"

He whistled when we told him.

"You'll get through all right," he said. "I'll see you in Quesnel. I am going there in a week or two to dig 50 pounds of gold. No use going for anything less."

"How far is it from the Fraser River to Barkerville?"

"Sixty miles," he told us. "But when you get halfway over, even part way, you will swear you have gone 120 miles already. You will ask in your prayers that you will meet men more honest than I am."

Our camp that night was beside the turgid Fraser at a point where the load of glacial silt was so thick that it swirled like fog when we drew a pail of water from it. The area was rich in grass but beset with sandflies, which chewed our horses raw and made eczema-like sores around their head and throat. We were up at 4:30 the next morning, rubbing the horses' sore spots with bacon grease saved for the purpose, and then were away by 7:30.

But now we had a new worry. Smoke appeared, turning the sky into a sheet of slate over which the sun slid dimly like a copper coin, and the valley walls became almost invisible. There was nothing we wanted less than a forest fire when we were about to set out on a wilderness trail of which nothing but evil had been spoken. But there were compensations, some edible, some amusing. Millions of raspberries, for example. Then there was the black bear who did not see us until we were almost upon him; he was so alarmed that he rolled down the embankment and galloped into the forest, hind feet up around his ears.

The railway tracks crossed three deep narrow canyons, little better than three cracks in the rock. Over one of these we took the horses on the railway trestle, the other two we negotiated down the steep walls of the canyons, and up again. We met two bearded young men with heavy packs who had come out of the Cariboo on the Goat River trail. They were less than enthusiastic about the Cariboo or the trail into it.

We came upon a trio of men — obviously the section crew — with their handcar off the rails, eating their lunch.

In reply to our questions the foreman said, "Yes, the tunnel is about a mile away. There are no trains scheduled so it will be safe to go through. The only danger is that there might be a special."

This unpleasant possibility made the black opening in the mountainside seem even darker when we faced it a half-hour later. As we approached, we looked for an alternative path over the mountain but there was none. The river flowed swiftly below, and rock faces above forbade passage. On the narrow ledge blasted out for the rails we stopped, tightened packs and discussed strategy.

"Just keep the horses moving," I told Ruth. "And if you hear a train coming, run for it!"

It might not have been very good advice, but I didn't have any better. It was a tense moment.

Calling to the packhorses, I rode quickly to the tunnel mouth, Dream following close behind. The other two packhorses attempted to turn back, but were met by Ruth's commanding shouts and whistling, and her persuading lariat rope — by now she needed no lessons in handling horses — and hard on our heels, the reluctant two entered the blackness. It was almost completely dark, only enough light filtering in behind us to illuminate the shiny surfaces of the rails. They looked like two threads leading into a bottomless black pool. Occasionally a horseshoe struck a spark and it flashed like lightning, then the tunnel went back to even greater darkness. For a few moments we lost all sense of direction. Our only guide was a slight movement of air from the far end. Then ahead a faint glow appeared and the rails again looked like illuminated threads, this time leading to light and escape. And at last there appeared a hole in the wall of darkness through which we could see light. Five sets of hooves began moving faster as we hurried to the opening and out into the daylight.

Five or six miles farther on, our pulse rates back to normal, we came to where a small river flowed in from the south. A sign said GOAT RIVER and a little cabin, which we had been told was part of the forestry service chain, sat just off the track. Not only wandering packhorse groups, but the provincial government borrowed the only access route through the country.

At this point we were supposed to leave the railway and plunge into the mountains, which we did, and found ourselves in a dark forest of huge trees under which there was no grass. Having already put in a long day we turned back to the abundant grass along the railway tracks and, picketing each horse, made camp for the night.

Tonight we would rest. Tomorrow we would start running the gauntlet, the ungentle Goat River trail.

That evening the fire warden, Hale, putted along the tracks on a little gasoline go-cart, stopped for a few minutes at the cabin and then came over to our camp.

The forest fire, he said, was about 50 miles distant and no threat to us.

Yes, we were the third party to "attempt" the trail. I felt there was a note of doubt in that phrase. He could have said that the other people had "gone through" on the trail. But of course, he really didn't know for sure if the previous travellers had actually got through.

Previous to this year the trail hadn't been used since 1913, which took it back to railway construction days. Did it ever get used to bring bootleg liquor to the railway camps? Not likely. The trail was too rough for such valuables. Besides, it was easier to get the liquor downstream on a raft or upstream on a sternwheeler.

"And those camps weren't Sunday-school picnics," Hale talked as he quietly studied our outfit. "There were the inevitable bootleggers and professional women and sharpies, and the safety valve was sure popping when payday rolled around. The towns weren't much but they got painted red."

Did they ever mine gold on the Goat River? Yes, indeed. A lot of gold. Nobody knows how much, because some that was dug out of the Goat was credited with being Barkerville gold. And about half the gold found anywhere was not reported in order to avoid paying tax.

"There are some miners at a cabin about eight miles up the trail," he said. "It would be a good idea to stop and get any information they might be able to give about the country ahead."

Hale had never been up the Goat River but he had a fund of knowledge of the Cariboo and a gift for words that painted vivid pictures with every sentence.

We had been elbowing against the Cariboo ever since we left the Tête Jaune Cache, he said, for there she was, the Cariboo, perched like a great castle on those mountains south of the Fraser River. In fact the Fraser, with its tributaries the Thompson and the North Thompson, makes a moat all the way around the Cariboo except for a small corner in the northeast where Canoe River drains out of those high mountains by Valemount.

High, thunderhead-high, he described the country. Full of snow for nine months and horseflies for the other three. Fish country. Salmon, all the way from the ocean, spawn in there. A good fur country too. For a long time it looked as if fur was the only cash crop to come out of there.

"Then they discovered gold and gold became king. It built towns in there and enough people came that they had to build roads into the towns. And then the mines played out and the people used the roads to move out, and the towns sank back into the gravel again."

"All but Barkerville. It's still there, half-full of people who believe the Cariboo is going to boom again. Some of them make more money out of trapping than they do out of mining, but they believe gold is going to be king again. Maybe they're right."

"Take old Fred Wells. Mined in the Kootenays. Brought the Surf Inlet mine into being. Thought there was more gold in the Cariboo, the motherlode, than had ever been taken out. He thought it would be quartz instead of placer. He found it, too, he did, on Cow Mountain. The book experts, the engineers and a lot of smart alecks had all said he was crazy, that he didn't know what he was talking about but he showed them. Ah yes, he showed them."

"He's 73 this year. I read about him in the paper the other day. He was born in 1860 and came across the Rockies when he was 22 with packhorses and Indians, before the CPR was through. And he's still going strong."

We asked about any old trails from the Upper Fraser into the Cariboo, remembering that the Overlanders had attempted a direct entry after the crossing by the one party at Tête Jaune Cache — and that we had once entertained ideas of a similar attempt.

"Back in 1871 the country was explored by the CPR for a railway pass that would lead across country from Tête Jaune to the mouth of the Quesnel River … " Hale had become the historian, and had an audience, sometimes a rare thing in his occupation, and he was now in full voice. "Somebody had spread the story around that there was a good route through from Barkerville by way of the lakes and Dominion Pass and down Castle River, just east of where McBride now sits. In August of that year a pack train of 50 horses and 22 men left Barkerville under a surveyor named

Mahood — James A. Mahood. They took the west and north side of the rectangle of lakes up there. At one stage they had to hack their way through dense jungle and swim their horses in the lake to get around a couple of rocky headlands, and when they left the lakes they had to corduroy muskegs and cut trail in rocky hillsides with pick and shovel.

"The top of the pass was high and glacier-capped, and they had to chisel a passage for the horses with picks and axes. They got out of the pass by the end of August, but the packers figured there was danger of being snowed in and threatened to desert the supplies and return to Barkerville. They were persuaded to stay ... and the snow did come and they didn't get to the Fraser until nearly the end of November."

"So much snow? This time of the year?" I interrupted with a feeling of consternation, for today, the 26th, was perilously close to the end of August.

"Yes. That's right. There's some real high mountains in the Cariboo Range in the northeast corner behind Valemount. Some nine-, ten-, eleven-thousand-foot peaks, and when the clouds from the Pacific have to climb over these they just dump their load of water and it comes down as snow. Sometimes when we are having a nice warm September day down here a blizzard is raging up there.

"But this Dominion Pass route with its steep grades and the need for a two-mile tunnel to get under the glacier at the top was proved worthless for railway purposes or anything else. They lost a lot of the horses they started out with.

"They were close enough to this Goat River trail to spit into it, but they never even took a look at it. Maybe they considered it an impossible trail. Maybe those that knew figured it was good gold country and were trying to keep others out of it."

"You are quite an historian," I said.

"I like hunting out local history," he replied. "I've got long evenings alone most of the time, and reading history and searching out old stories is better than going crazy."

The smoke was still with us next morning when we awoke and discovered Rex had broken his picket rope and wandered a mile or so back along the track.

Hale came from his cabin whilst we were eating breakfast and presented us with a pair of good packing boxes to replace the ones O'Hara had worn on his roll in Tonquin. The typewriter and mirror were miraculously unbroken, though the boxes were almost totally destroyed.

He then hauled a notebook from his pocket, and, with pencil poised, said he would like to know something about us, just in case somebody inquired. As he finished his notes I caught a glimpse of him adding to Ruth's description "pretty" and to mine "like a college professor."

"So you're both 22," he said, "and married two months. You've got a lot ahead of you. Get on with it!"

He shook hands with us, got on his putter and disappeared toward McBride.

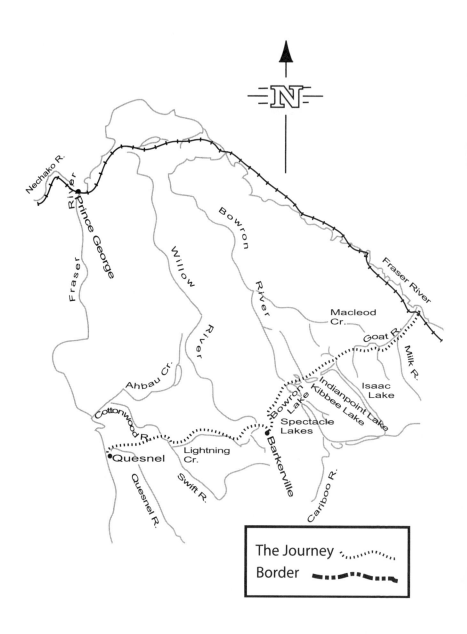

The Journey ⋯⋯⋯⋯

Border ▬·▬·▬·▬

Over the Goat River Trail to Quesnel

Having decided we were only going to the miners' camp eight miles distant, we let the horses rest and made a leisurely noon departure.

Up over the rim of mountains above us lay the lofty Cariboo. The staircase we had to climb to attain it was the Goat River trail, and we were on it.

It was not immediately obvious that this was reason for congratulations. It was dusk in the tall forest. Huge cedar trees, six feet in diameter, rose hundreds of feet in the air and while these immense columns were limbless for many feet from the ground, their upper foliage joined to shut out the sky and much of the light. About six feet from the ground a waxy layer of leaves on tall stems created a carpet from which arose sprigs of bright red berries. The addition of an occasional clump of symmetrically spreading ferns completed a picture of tremendous beauty. It could have been a carving, or a painting, for apart from us, there was no sound or motion. But the beauty was marred by the fact that these waxy green plants were Devil's Club with sharp spines on every inch of the stems on the underpart of every leaf, even on the roots wherever they were exposed. So cruel were these that the horses could not be forced against them.

Several of the trees had fallen across the trail in such places as to make climbing round them impossible. Previous travellers had built ramps on either side of the six-foot obstructions by laying fallen limbs and lesser trees parallel with the trunks, enabling horses to scramble over them. From the top of these we could look in so far that the brown trunks formed a line of phantoms against further vision.

"Surely it's the Devil's Cathedral," murmured Ruth.

We built two sets of ramps against new-fallen trunks, ascended out of this eerie forest and went down a canyon on a wall of blue clay so steep that the horses were on their haunches much of the time. Then we clawed our way up the other side. Underfoot, the trail had turned to boulders overlaid with squishy humus mud, and nearby raspberry bushes offered fat berries, but the threat of rain, felt more than seen, was in the air and we pushed on.

Soon we came to a clearing in which stood two cabins, one new, one old. Smoke was coming from the chimney of the new one, and a bearded, bespectacled man appeared at the door as we approached.

"Yes, this is Boulder Camp, last outpost of civilization on the Goat River trail. There is some grass down by the stream, and there's the other cabin you can use if you wish. It does look like rain."

The cabin was swept out, our little stove erected and stove pipes thrust into the low tin chimney. The horses had been put down on the scant pasture, bars placed to stop wandering, and we hoped that if the rain was coming, it would come now, while we were under a roof. We planned to stop over.

The next day followed what had become our pattern for a day off the trail — a little more leisure in rising, a little longer for breakfast, rigging to be repaired, baking and laundering to be done, diaries to be written. It was a dark lowering day, the clouds swirling around the treetops, and we enjoyed the roof over our heads and the heat of the cabin around us, and, in this lone land, the sight of three men occasionally coming and going ... neighbours.

We visited them in the evening. There were two brothers, George Fraser, from Vancouver, his brother Simon — "not the original

Simon Fraser, of course" — and a third, Louis Burnell, the latter two from Kamloops.

Louis, lean, muscular and black-bearded, had scoured the surrounding hills for three years searching for gold, and, according to the Frasers, knew the country as well as any man.

"Tell them about the Goat River trail," said George.

"I've never heard it discussed in polite language," Louis replied, looking at Ruth. "Profanity is the only suitable one for that trail."

"But it's not impossible. Two outfits have gone through this year." He took paper and pencil and started sketching a map, showing streams and unusual rock formations. "Boulder Camp here is the end of what might be called a good trail." Ruth and I shuddered at the memory of what the "good" trail was, and wondered what an indescribable trail might be. Louis, that very afternoon, had gone to the railway for mail and returned in less than two hours, a trip that had taken us three and a half hours. We listened to him.

"From here on, the trail is of little practical value, except to keep you in the general direction you want to go. I've never travelled it with horses, but afoot it's hell for mud and steepness and Devil's Club."

On his map he sketched in steep places, grassy spots and stream crossings.

"I've only been to the top of the watershed — Macleod River, that is — but this side, the Goat River watershed, is bad enough even in dry weather. God help you if it rains!"

He handed me the map with an expression that wordlessly said that from now on, it was a matter between God and us, and that he, Louis Burnell, had done all he could.

"Now tell us about your trip," one of the Frasers suggested.

After an hour, during which biscuits had been baked and served with jam and tea, George Fraser sat back with a sigh of relief.

"You know," he said, "you will make it through the Goat River country. Ever since I saw you yesterday I've been trying to figure out a way to stop you. But not now. You'll get through!"

"Now tell them what you called them when they rode into the clearing yesterday," his brother urged. "Or will I?"

"All right, I'll confess," George agreed, looking embarrassed. "I said, 'if there was ever a pair of babes in the woods, here they are'."

These men, the Frasers, spent part of each summer here and extracted enough wheat-sized nuggets "to pay wages," and Louis spent from spring thaw until freeze-up at it.

They were already astir when we arose the next morning. Their actions as soon as we appeared caused me to think they had been discussing ways and means of helping these "babes in the woods" on their way, for when we brought the horses up from their canyon pasture they looked them over carefully and bathed two saddle sores with warm salty water, found some horseshoes and did a really professional job of shoeing two feet that were bare and would have become dangerously sore. Then they helped pack.

When we were about ready to step into our saddles Simon called from the cabin door to come and have a cup of tea. The modest cup of tea grew, western style, into a full meal at which we were urged to eat and eat.

It started to rain as, mounted and with slickers fastened to our chins, we finally said our goodbyes. For the first time on the trip we felt a premonition of evil amounting almost to fear. We were going into territory of which no one spoke well.

Immediately out of the small clearing, however, there was no time for premonitions. Within a hundred feet of the miners' cabin the trail, hidden at the start by heavy brush, dropped suddenly to stream level. The horses plummeted down, and from that moment on either one horse or another was in trouble. The trail led for a distance across a steep slope of blue clay in which the horses tugged and wrenched and wallowed. Swamp holes from marshes coming down the mountain required courage in crossing. When the trail led through a spruce swamp on steep slopes and the spruce roots stood out as slippery traps, it was almost impossible for horses to keep their feet under them. But the worst was when we crossed a swamp on a hillside that had been corduroyed in the distant past, and the corduroy had sunk in on the lower side and pushed up on the upper to such a degree that we could only let each horse pick its careful way across, an inch at a time. There were frequent falls and scrambles to get back up. Once O'Hara fell and rolled so that all four feet were in the air and we thought we would have to roll him farther down the hill, and then cut his pack to get him up, but somehow he managed to regain his feet.

What with crashing through bushes and helping struggling horses, we were both soaking wet five minutes after our start, so that by the time we had crossed the glacial surge of Milk River and come upon the grass, we made camp. It was, according to Louis' map, five miles from Boulder Camp. It had taken us four strenuous hours. When we unpacked, O'Hara stood with legs apart, groaning and grinding his teeth, ill from something, we supposed, he had eaten at Boulder Camp. When his pack was off he rolled and rolled, groaning horribly. We felt sure his death was imminent.

We were erecting the tent when the tinkling of a bell down-trail made us wonder if we were hearing things. But soon a rider appeared, followed by a large police dog and a packhorse with a bell. His horses, the big red sorrel he was riding and the cream buckskin under the pack, were in good shape. As he rode up he put a rifle in the scabbard under his knee.

He was George Wilcox, from the Peace River country. He had seen us at Red Pass junction, the other side of Tête Jaune Cache, and having learned of our intention to go through to Barkerville, had tried ever since to catch us.

"I'd like to tag along with you," he said. "A broken leg in this country would be just as fatal as a broken neck."

He made camp, a bivouac of canvas, close enough for us to hear him carrying on a running conversation with his dog while he built a huge fire and cooked a huge supper. His rifle was always within reach.

"I've been told this is bad bear country," he said. "There's lots of fish and lots of woods, and not enough people to teach bears respect."

We had noticed that everyone we had seen west of McBride was armed almost like banditti. Over the top, in the Cariboo, not many miles away, lay a huge quadrangle of lakes, a tremendous spawning ground for salmon and an equally attractive feeding area for bears. Within the area of the lakes, the Bowron Lake Game Reserve, established in 1925, offered the same bears refuge from hunters. Wilcox kept the bell on his horse to notify bears of his presence, his dog to give the alert and his rifle always in hand or within reach.

"And that goddam trail ... " — profanity did not abash him — " ... from the miners' cabin to here is the longest jeesly five miles in North America. And dirty, jeesly dirty. Somebody told me that when you get partway in you'd keep going because you wouldn't have the guts to go back over the trail again. That's me!"

Heavy rains next day held us all in camp. O'Hara was on his feet again and eating, but all the horses were humpbacked against the rain and obviously miserable, and the grass was disappearing.

The following morning, it was still raining and everyone was soaked before packing was done; nevertheless we set out.

This would be a day to illustrate the limits to which humans and horses might go and still survive.

Just out of camp, a series of bogs challenged us. Rex got down so badly in one hole that we had to unpack him before he could get out. When we could, we used the gravel bars of the river, until falls or fast water forced us to the hillsides. Here we worked a perilous passage up and down steep lateral gullies and scrambled across near-perpendicular slopes, the horses picking their way among slippery roots.

Confronted with a series of frothing waterfalls, we scouted ahead on foot. The trail was almost hidden under mud, moss and forest rubbish, but we saw that it followed a ledge scarcely wide enough to accommodate the packs, and that we would all be drenched with spray and nearly deafened by the roar of water vibrating in confined space.

Into this bedlam we led the horses one at a time. Their legs trembled as they inched through the confusion of noise, water and pouring rain. In this perilous situation even O'Hara accepted human advice and encouragement, and at last all seven had reached comparative safety above the cataracts.

Ruth remembered Louis Burnell's words at Boulder Camp, "God help you if it rains," and added that we had just had a demonstration of the power of prayer.

We had a brief reprieve on river gravel, and were then forced over another ridge and down a long rocky slide with a three-foot drop at the bottom. This was one of several places where it seemed impossible that horses could be taken in the opposite direction. After a bit of gravel-bar travelling, we were forced to the mountainside again on a narrow steep slope where low bushes and conifer growth hid slippery tree roots. I was leading on Dick when suddenly he fell, twisting my leg. He scrambled up and then fell again, apparently into space. I half-fell, half-leaped out of the saddle and rolled down the mountain, expecting the horse to come down on top of me. When a tree stopped me, I looked up and saw Dick climbing out of the hidden wash that had undermined the trail and caused his fall.

The packhorses were approaching the hidden trap, and I shouted a warning.

"What in the world are you doing down there?" asked Ruth and then saw the pained look on my face. My knee was hot and numb but not broken, and the rest of the party got through in safety.

An hour later we crossed what we thought was the Macleod River, found good grass and camped.

In the late evening several reverberations rolled down from Mount Macleod, to the west of us. We supposed it was somebody blasting for gold, and next day, in a confusion of game trails, we found and followed for a short distance a freshly blazed trail leading up the mountain. We made little progress that day but were fairly sure we were on the right trail, because the later blazes were old and the stream we were following flowed in the direction it should, according to our maps.

It rained that evening, just after we had hurriedly erected the tent, and the water stood out in a thick film on the inside of the canvas. For the first time in our entire trip we could not find dry wood for the stove, or get dry before we went to bed.

During the night we were awakened by the sound of an animal screaming. We listened, heard George put more wood on his fire, and went to sleep again. In the morning we asked him if he had heard the noise.

Yes, he had. His horses had wanted to come and share the fire with him.

"Cougar, I guess," he said.

It had snowed in the night, flakes as big as saucers, which melted almost as soon as they fell. On the mountains around us the snowline was down to within 500 feet of our level.

Later in the day, going down a gully, we came upon two young men cooking some food alongside the trail. They were four days out of Barkerville, hoped to get to the rails at the mouth of Goat River that night and were aghast to learn how long we had taken to cover the distance.

We exchanged trail information and then continued our fight with bog, fallen timber, steep slopes and Devil's Club. About the middle of the afternoon Wilcox suggested we stop and light a fire to warm up, and since we were all cold and soaking wet, we did. It was good. Continuing, we came within sight of a lake, turned from it, spent an hour in an abomination of fallen timber and returned to the lake again. We plunged along the shore for a while, and in gathering dusk made camp by a handful of grass.

The next morning the sound of horse bells was missing. At first we thought the animals had back-trailed, and we were indignant; then we discovered them standing idle, too discouraged to nibble at even the few blades of grass that were there.

Our lead mount, Dick, caused us concern. His eyes were deep blue and staring, one sunken.

Wilcox now suggested that he go ahead; he could travel faster than our trail-worn horses to the next grass, and there he would wait for us. We agreed and he pulled out, 15 minutes before we left.

Although Ruth and Cliff sometimes have to round up their animals when the latter take a notion to head back to the prairies, the courage, intelligence and loyalty of good packhorses have solved many a problem and maybe even saved some lives.

That day the trail was one of confusion and fallen timber, and we no longer had any help from our most dependable horse, Dick. He refused to take even low fallen timbers, and, to help him, in detours, we got off the trail and plunged through even worse going.

Struggling back to the trail with great difficulty, we went down to a lake, lost the trail again, then returned to where we thought we had seen a branch trail. Here Dick refused to cross a log two feet high, indicating to us there was no trail the other side of the log.

For a few moments we milled around in confusion. The forest got darker, the air got colder, the mountains higher and more confusing. Suddenly we were lost.

Then we saw a man sitting on a log, resting his pack, his rifle butt on the log and pointing to the sky. He was calmly watching us.

Yes, we were on the trail, all right, bad as it seemed.

"Go down to the lake," he said. "I saw your tracks there, where you turned around, and I wondered at it. Then follow the edge of the lake, sometimes right in the water, which is not deep. Go between Kibbee Lakes, and in about 28 miles you will come to a wagon road, then in another five to a car road, which will lead you out to civilization."

With that he waved us on our way, and walking around the horses, disappeared along the trail. We never knew his name.

The directions he had given were explicit and correct. We tramped along the shallow waters of the lake, followed the trail and left high mountains and straining climbs behind. For the first time since we left the railway tracks so many wet days ago, the sun came out.

But now Dick, carrying only an empty saddle except when we had to walk in water, refused to cross even a foot-high fallen log. If I stopped when I was leading him, he continued walking and bumped into me. I looked at his eyes. The pupils had dilated greatly, leaving great vacant pools. The horse was almost entirely blind.

We came to a large meadow with a locked cabin, then to another meadow and an unlocked cabin with a table, a bunk and a stove. We could ask no more.

That evening, getting warm and dry, we enjoyed watching the lake as the moon rose and laid a pathway of silver between two spruce trees from the near shore to the distant mountain. Loons called and fish splashed to complete a picture in wonderful contrast to the harsh wilderness we had come through. We discovered we were not yet surfeited with mountain beauty.

The horses were better for the feed and the dry night; even Dick seemed stronger. We rearranged packs, throwing away our worst pair of boxes so that all camp effects could go on Dream and O'Hara. Dick carried only a blanket and an empty packsaddle.

We moved about six miles that day and stopped only because Dick finally refused to go another step. We had just passed a meadow, so decided to return to it. Dick had repeatedly tried to turn back, and now we found he would willingly back-trail. Shortly we were in a beautiful little spot beside a lodge-type of structure — somebody's wilderness retreat — and camped where a little stream poured into a lake. Again that evening, moonbeams painted a silvery path into the purple haunts of loons, and we heard the splash of leaping fish.

In the little stream, three fish, each about two feet long, breasted the current but did not rise to my efforts with a hook.

Had we managed to catch one, it might have changed our program. Inventory of our pack boxes showed we were out of food save for a few pounds of cornmeal, a can or two of milk, some coffee and a fistful of sugar. We could dally no longer. At the same time we would do our utmost to get Dick to a ranch where he would be looked after.

The next day we came to where the road became wide enough for cars. A group of men were making repairs to a bridge and we asked them if they knew a rancher who might adopt a horse.

Half a mile farther on we came to a chalet-type home where a lady came to the door in response to our knock, and listened to our story. Then she called her husband.

We asked John Wendle if we could leave our sick horse with him, and told him of some of Dick's virtues.

"Yes, bring him in through the gate and turn him loose," the man said. "We'll look after him and when you send for him or come for him, you can have him."

So the packsaddle was taken off Dick, and he was led through the gate and the halter removed. At the friendly slap of dismissal on his shoulder, he walked slowly into the field and started to eat. The courage and intelligence of that animal had solved many of our problems, maybe saved our lives. He had given us everything he had. There were tears in our eyes and lumps in our throats when we mounted our horses.

Now Rex was the lead saddle horse, followed closely by Dream.

It was 18 miles to Barkerville, and we hoped to make most of this distance before camping. We passed a sawmill where a number of men were working, and half a mile down the road a smiling Chinese man invited us into the cookhouse. The cup of coffee, accompanied by several slices of apple pie, cake and doughnuts, was ambrosia indeed, after our menu of cornmeal porridge in the morning and cornmeal cakes at night.

"You have come far?" he asked, and when we told him, he whistled softly. "And up the Goat River trail? It used to be said that if you survived a trip through the Goat River you could ride a rock slide down a mountain."

The next morning we got to Barkerville.

Picketed on a grassy slope just outside the town, a pair of familiar-looking horses — a big red sorrel and a cream buckskin — drew our attention, and we rode over to discover George Wilcox crouched beside a big fire cooking a big meal. He had arrived yesterday and was looking for a job.

"This is no poor man's rush," he said. "My gold-pan is going to be used for a dish pan from now on. If I don't get a job by the time I eat all my grub, I'll sell my horses and head back for the Peace River country."

He had had one good feed since leaving us. He had shot three fish in a small stream and bagged five grouse almost immediately after, then camped for two days while he and his dog had eaten the meat.

We left him, and, riding on, came in about half a mile to where a village of tents set upon the gravel of the valley floor announced the resurging gold capital of British Columbia: Barkerville. The first tents were entirely of canvas and appeared to have been newly erected; the next group, a little older, had wooden floors and sides. These gave way in turn to old log structures with shake roofs. Then there was a lumberyard and Saint Saviour's Church, which had been built in 1870 and now served as a school. There were log buildings that looked as if they had grown from the ground, fruited and were now returning to it. There were frame buildings nudging each other with their board sidings dried and twisted from three score paint-less summers. Still farther along the road, business establishments fronted onto sidewalks that changed levels with each building, with steps leading up at one edge and down at the other as the need required. Steps led from store porches to the street gravel, and occasionally the porches were extended in narrow, pier-like walks, probably to enable passengers to enter on porch level into the stagecoaches that once operated here. Old signs on the weathered buildings indicated that in this one a bath might be had, in another one meals, and in yet others, a bed. The old grey buildings looked just as the miners had left them before the turn of the century.

This was the second Barkerville. The first one had risen like a cluster of mushrooms around the Billy Barker claim, and in September 1868 had caught fire when an amorous miner knocked out a stovepipe while trying to kiss a girl. In two hours, 116 buildings were burned and the population left homeless. But rebuilding a better Barkerville started the next morning.

The flamboyant glory of Barkerville was soon overshadowed by the Klondike — but it never quite became a ghost town. By 1930 the population had dwindled to about 200 people.

The news of Fred Wells' quartz discovery on Cow Mountain triggered a rush in the winter of 1932–33. Not all the search was for quartz, but much was renewed for placer deposits. Claims were staked in six feet of snow; airplanes were used to get people where they wanted to stake claims. Some put claims on the graveyard, exhibiting even greater enthusiasm than they had in the 19th century. Now, influenced by Fred Wells' discovery and development, the town started rising again. It had four stores, two hotels, a post office, a telegraph office, two churches, four or five cafés and a new police station. On the only street, right-hand-drive vehicles of pre-20s vintage parked alongside shiny limousines of 1933. Grizzled veterans and one long-skirted old lady mingled with short-skirted secretaries and white-shirted businessmen.

There was no talk of depression here. A boom had hit last December and now the post office served 1,200 adults, and the man behind the wicket expected this to be only the beginning. Wages were about $4.50 a day and living costs about a third of that. People were optimistic and happy, so happy ... and so busy that a political meeting held last week had attracted only six of the townsfolk.

Barkerville rose like a cluster of mushrooms around the Billy Barker claim, but its flamboyant glory was soon overshadowed by the Klondike.

As we sat our horses for a few minutes at the upper end of the street, under the scrutiny of St. Saviour's Church, Barkerville seemed to be rising for the third time to be the birthplace of legends, the brightest spot in British Columbia. In its heyday it had been the gold capital of the world, the centre of a region where, it was boasted, gold dust was so abundant it could be panned out of the moss, where men scooped from the gravel gold to the value of a thousand dollars a day and there was no limit to people's belief in its future. They said Vancouver would never amount to anything because it was so far from Barkerville.

Within a few miles of here, men had endured in the 1860s the long hard winters at high elevations, living in holes in the snow in order to hold the claims they had staked.

Here and in the neighbouring communities, Chief Justice Matthew Baillie Begbie, travelling by stagecoach, saddle horse or sometimes afoot, meted out stern British justice. He was called the Hanging Judge by the white man and Rope Tyee by the Indian. Whether he deserved these names or not is debatable, but it is never denied that the judge, dispensing swift justice without fear or favour, maintained law and order and prevented the drift of mining towns into lawlessness and a reign of vigilantes.

Here indeed, attracted by the gold of the Fraser and the Cariboo, enough men of British and Canadian loyalties came, and enough stayed, to establish claims to make the area truly British Columbia and check the possibility of annexation by the United States.

There were many stories of life in the goldfields, but the one most often told concerned John A. Cameron, who was known as "Cariboo" Cameron. Arriving in Victoria from Ontario in February of 1862 with his wife and baby daughter, Cameron suffered a heavy blow when the child died within a week. Then a chance meeting with Robert Stevenson, an Ontario acquaintance, led to a partnership that took Cameron and his beautiful wife to the goldfields. At first they acted as suppliers to the miners, then Cameron staked a claim and struck it rich. But his wife died of typhoid. She had hated the creeks, and her dying wish was to

Known as the Hanging Judge, Chief Justice Matthew Baillie Begbie travelled by stagecoach, saddle horse and on foot to mete out stern British justice.

be buried in Ontario, and Cameron, who blamed himself for her death and the baby's, determined to fulfil her request. Placing her body first in a tin coffin and then in a wooden one, he interred her in a deserted cabin, where she rested from October 1862 until the new year. The temperature at the time was minus 30° F. On the last day of January 1863, Cameron, his friend Stevenson and some others started out over the high plateau between Richfield and Williams Creek. They travelled on snowshoes and pulled a toboggan on which the casket had been lashed, together with blankets, food, a 50-pound sack of gold and a two-gallon jug of Hudson's Bay rum. The temperature fell to 50 below zero, they ran out of food, the jug of rum rolled down a hill, hit a tree and knocked the cork out, losing its contents, and they had difficulty in following the trail. All the men except Cameron and Stevenson had dropped out by the time they reached Lac La Hache. A smallpox epidemic was raging and in many of the communities there were more dead people than alive, with the dead buried in the snow or left unburied in tents. They bought three horses, one after the other, to pull the sled, and two died of cold and hardship. At Port Douglas they boarded a river steamer and five weeks after leaving Cameron's cabin in the goldfields they arrived in Victoria. Here he had the coffin filled with alcohol and, following a funeral service attended by 800 wintering miners, he again buried his wife's body.

He then returned to his claim.

In late fall, once more in Victoria, this time with $350,000 as his summer's earnings, he took the casket to New York and thence to Cornwall, Ontario, where the body had a third funeral service and a third burial.

But now sinister imaginations and malicious tongues started the rumour that the coffin did not contain the body but was full of gold for which he had sold his wife to an Indian chief. In horror, sorrow and disgust Cameron had the casket lifted and opened to show the perfectly preserved body to his wife's parents and friends, whereupon she was buried for the fourth time.

The story of John "Cariboo" Cameron and his wife Sophia, the "Beauty of Barkerville," is a tragic one. Sophia died of typhoid, and John fulfilled his promise to her to bury her in her native Ontario, but only after overcoming incredible obstacles.

Cameron tried to restart his life. He married again and built a beautiful home for his wife, in which they lived happily. He gave his brothers farms and established one for himself and invested in various businesses. But the farm proved unproductive and the businesses disastrous, and finally, having lost his fortune, he went back to the goldfields. But this time success did not smile upon him, and when he died in 1888 he was penniless. Even the town that had grown up around the Cameron claim and was called Camerontown also gradually sank back into the gravel or merged with Barkerville.

Barkerville, a companion town to Camerontown, which lived on where others disappeared, was named for Billy Barker, an ex-sailor who had jumped ship and come to the Cariboo. He had sunk a shaft below the canyon on Williams Creek where all the experienced miners said there was no possibility of finding gold. Below 50 feet, deeper than any other shaft had yet been sunk, he and his partners struck pay dirt that yielded 1,000 dollars to a foot of gravel.

A town of shafts grew up around the shaft. Barker, suddenly a rich man, married a widow in Victoria, a woman with such extravagant tastes and a thirst for gay living that he spent his money faster than the mine could produce it, and when in 1866 the mine ceased producing, he was broke. Ultimately a subscription was taken up for his stage fare to Victoria, where he died in 1894, penniless, in an old man's home.

Miners were a volatile lot, always ready to go any time the word "gold" was shouted, whispered or even hinted at. When they found gold they built a village, then tore the buildings down to mine the gravel where the buildings had stood. When the workings played out they moved, carrying with them what they could on their backs and leaving the rest, even sometimes the grave of a companion who had succumbed to illness or hardship.

We could have stayed longer, but it was a three-day trip to Quesnel and we were out of food.

When we said goodbye to Wilcox, we asked if he would return to the Peace River country over the Goat River trail if job hunting failed.

"Never again over that trail," he said. "Not for all the gold in these hills. Never!"

Camped that night 10 miles closer to Quesnel, we found that the estimated 45 miles from the Goat River siding on the railway had taken 12 days, including stopovers for weather and to rest the horses, and by the time we reached Quesnel three days later, we had lived on cornmeal (plus a lunch given us by a kindly Chinese person) for six consecutive days.

But the trip was interesting. When we laddered up the Goat River trail the seasons had changed from summer to autumn. Bright sunny days succeeded crisp nights. Grass was abundant and the trees were turning yellow and scarlet. Over this road, on which we now seemed the only pack train, there had undoubtedly been in the past more beasts of burden than wheeled vehicles. Even camels had been used for a while before they created too much disturbance among the other pack animals and were driven from the trails. With the road came lumbering teams of oxen and dashing, semi-wild teams of the stagecoaches hurtling their express and passengers and boxes of gold to their various destinations. Here too had passed packhorses, each loaded with 250 pounds of gold in 50-pound sacks, and herds of cattle being driven to the gold camps to supply miners with meat.

This had been a highway of high hopes and deep despair, for only a few who went in so hopefully came out with fortunes. Many returned to their eastern homes broken in purse and physique, and many were buried in the graveyard at Barkerville ... and some died who weren't buried.

Occasionally we were met or overtaken by a car, and our packhorses, unaccustomed to yielding right-of-way to anyone, showed their disapproval.

All the while we were leaving the high mountains behind and traversing a tremendous plateau of sombre spruce. Over all rose a great inverted bowl of blue that moved forever westward with us, a bowl from which bright sun shone in the daytime and almost equally bright moon beamed at night.

One evening — and we detected that the days were now much shorter — we rode until dusk before finding a campsite, then slept like dead people, to discover next morning a grave with an ancient weather-beaten cross only 50 feet from our tent.

We wondered if the occupant had been going to the goldfields or had been on his way out. Then, around a corner, we came to Quesnel. We had been on the trail 12 weeks.

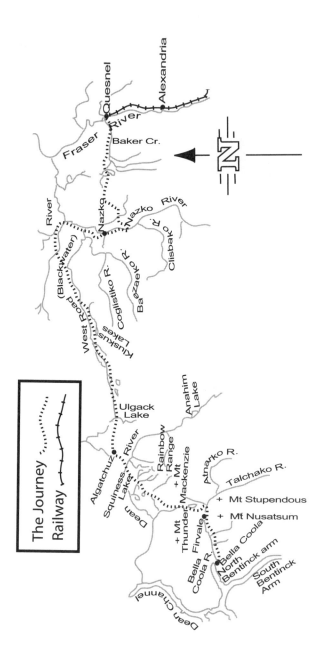

The Journey
Railway

Alexandria

Quesnel

Fraser River

Baker Cr.

N

Nazko

Nazko River

Clisbako R.

Bazaeko R.

Coglistiko R.

River

(Blackwater)

West Road

Kluskus Lakes

Ulgack Lake

Anahim Lake

Algatchuz Lake

Squiness River

Rainbow Range

+ Mt Mackenzie

Atnarko R.

Talchako R.

+ Mt Stupendous

+ Mt Nusatsum

+ Mt Thunder

Dean

+ Mt Finvale

Bella Coola R.

Bella Coola

North Bentinck arm

South Bentinck Arm

Dean Channel

QUESNEL TO BELLA COOLA

Quesnel, on a little flat at the junction of the Quesnel and Fraser rivers, didn't seem as full of rushing and reminiscences as Barkerville, but that might have been an illusion caused by the wide streets and orderly layout of the town. While Barkerville's growth had been haphazard, Quesnel was laid out by the Royal Engineers in 1863, who foresaw that it would become the distribution centre of the Cariboo. Seventy years earlier Alexander Mackenzie had found an Indian encampment there, and remarked that wild onions growing in the neighbourhood had had a disastrous effect on their supplies by increasing the men's appetites. In 1808, Simon Fraser had camped there and named the clear river after his lieutenant, Jules Maurice Quesnel.

For a while, Alexandria, the depot and transshipping point for furs and goods to and from New Caledonia, was the important fur trade centre. It was there, lower down the river, that Mackenzie turned back on his tracks and determined to go overland to the Pacific. Quesnel sprang into being when gold was discovered, as a meeting point at the junction of two gold-rich streams. In 1860 two stores appeared, and when the Overlanders arrived in 1862, Quesnel was recognized as a main entry to the goldfields. In 1863 the sternwheel steamer *Enterprise*, built at Soda Creek, started making regular runs between there and Quesnel, initiating the amazing saga of steamboating on the Upper Fraser and eventually serving the 500-mile run between Tête Jaune Cache and Soda

Creek until 1920. During that period Quesnel was at various times a shipbuilding centre, a packhorse town and a railhead.

In 1864 six Indians accused of implication in the Chilcotin War were tried for murder in Quesnel and four of them were sentenced by Judge Begbie to be hanged. A huge crowd witnessed the event, and a rumour still persists that the Indians were bribed with a sack of flour to attend, and the Cariboo whites threw a party.

But when we rode into Quesnel we were more interested in food and mail than in history. A bundle of letters and some parcels containing cakes, cookies and candies from home awaited us at the post office, and we set up camp and turned the horses loose with the promise of three days' rest.

Ruth turned to me from one of her letters.

"We have an urgent invitation to go south and spend the winter in Vernon," she said. "They are worried about our getting caught by early snows."

There was some sense in the suggestion. Vernon was Ruth's hometown, and ahead, across the Fraser, lay 300 unknown miles and the Coast Range mountains between us and Bella Coola. And winter was coming on.

"How are you going to answer that?" I asked.

"You want to go to Bella Coola," she stated rather than asked. "I shall tell them we love them and not to worry because there is no danger." And that was that.

The screaming of a steam locomotive rang through the trees, reminding us we were once again on steel. The last time we could remember hearing a locomotive was at Moose Lake when it blasted the message to get off the track quickly — or else!

The whistle now ringing belonged to Pacific Great Eastern Railway, which first tooted into Quesnel in October 1921, bringing with it the realization that once again Quesnel was the end of transportation and the jumping-off place for wilderness destinations. Freight had come by river steamer and bull team, by packhorse and camel back, by fast B. X. stage and footslogging man. Now everything for the rancher, sawmiller and miner would come by rail. The last river steamer plying the Fraser discontinued operations just months before the coming of the railroad.

Quesnel had shared in many gold rushes. The first was to the mouth of her own river, the Quesnel, and when white stampeders moved to richer ground up the watershed, Chinese people took over the gravel bars of both the Quesnel and Fraser rivers. And then when the steamer *Enterprise* connected two segments of the Cariboo wagon road and made Quesnel the port for the Williams Creek mines, everything went through that town. It was a winter haven for miners, and when the mines were depleted, it speeded them on their way to other places. At first Lillooet was the departure point for northbound traffic, but when the CPR made Ashcroft an available railhead, freight and passengers rolled from there to Quesnel and points further on. In 1870–1871 a gold rush took place to the Omineca country, and in 1874 to the Cassiar, both passing through Quesnel. During the rush to the Yukon and the Klondike in 1898, thousands of men reached Quesnel by normal transportation, stopped overnight, then headed into the wilderness towards the northern goldfields.

In a few days we also would be leaving Quesnel, not for a goldfield, but for Bella Coola. As usual we tried to gather some information about the country ahead.

A Mr. Perry, who struck up acquaintance with us the first few minutes we were in Quesnel, told us we should see Paul Krestinuk, who had a "string of trading posts west of Quesnel." In fact, Mr. Perry not only told us of Paul Krestinuk, he arranged a meeting with him for us.

Paul's office was over a warehouse and unfurnished except for a plain desk and three or four chairs. Beside the desk an open window let in a gentle breeze and several bluebottle flies, which returned to bang against the glass the way they did in schoolrooms on the prairies. Outside the window was a tree with shiny red apples.

Yes, he had a trading post at Algatchuz [or Algatcho, now known as Ulkatcho] about 250 miles west of Quesnel. In the summer they serviced this post with team and wagon, in the winter with sleigh.

It would be impossible to lose this trail except in deep snow.

At Algatchuz, he said, the trail divided, one fork ascending the Dean River to Anahim Lake, then following the telegraph line through the mountains to Bella Coola. The other branch went across the Dean, climbed into the Coast Range and descended on the sides of canyons so steep, where the trails were so narrow, that if a horse ever fell you would never recover even the packsaddle.

No, he himself had only been as far as Algatchuz, but his Indian customers travelled the trail, and their numerous stories were always in the same vein.

"If you go across the Dean, get an Indian to guide you. The crossing is very dangerous."

The Indians in this country were numerous, white men rare. But the Indians were friendly and would supply you with fish and meat. They would not frown upon someone with writing purposes in mind.

"Tell them you write-um book," he advised specifically.

The Indians, said Paul, believed that anyone trading with them should be bald. Paul was far from being bald, but he close-cropped his hair in deference to the Indians' beliefs. They also believed he was the bringer of many good things in their lives. During one period of near-starvation caused by heavy storms, the Indian mothers told their little ones to pray that Paul would get through the windfall with food for the starving people. When he did get through, in time, they pointed out the effectiveness of prayer.

Yes indeed, the Indians were very friendly, because they were treated right and priests going into the country were given detailed instructions on how to act toward them.

(We wondered who instructed the priests but didn't ask.)

Paul Krestinuk had a partner, John Ward, now on his way in from Algatchuz. He would be here in a few days and would be turning right around as soon as he got his wagonload of trade goods. If we wanted, we could put our packs on the wagon and ride alongside. This way we could gather a great deal of information.

Or if we wished, Paul's partner at their first westerly post, Nazko, 60 miles distant, would get horses and show us through to Algatchuz.

To both these offers we smiled a negative reply, saying we preferred to travel at our own speed. The truth was we feared such services would cost money, and we hadn't any, except a small cheque from the *Calgary Herald*. But Paul's help was of great value. With shovel and axe, he had built this wagon road through the wilderness for almost 200 miles, and the road itself would be our guide.

Early on our third day in Quesnel we were aroused by the clanging of a large bell, such as our horses wore. Almost incredulous at the thought that they might have come into camp to be packed, I lifted the tent wall and looked out — right into the face of a cow. The cow wore the bell, had a full udder and was obviously ready for milking. Thinking that a bowl of fresh milk would be a welcome addition to our table, I slipped out in pyjamas and socks, with a large bowl and sweet words for Bossie. But at the sight of me, the cow backed up, and as I approached, she turned and fled, bell clanging in alarm.

Having run out of food on the leg of the journey just completed, we bought all we could, and when funds were exhausted, looked our outfit over for anything we might be able to do without. The third packsaddle and pair of angora goat-hair chaps, carried for cold weather, were selected.

"We should get 25 or 30 dollars for these," I said to Ruth as I set out for the second-hand shop we had noticed the day before.

But the dealer had other ideas.

"Five dollars for the chaps," he said, rolling a smoke nonchalantly as he spoke. "One dollar for the packsaddle. Times are hard around here. People make their own. Take it or leave it."

His offer was about 10 percent of the value of the goods, but we needed food.

Even more important than food were horseshoes, and some of this money was earmarked for them until the lucky find of a half-dozen useful shoes as we took a shortcut across some vacant lots solved the problem, and to that degree, our food problem.

We estimated it would take us four weeks to get to Bella Coola, but when we left Quesnel our two packhorses, Dream and O'Hara, carried supplies for six. Food, we had learned, was something more than a satisfaction for hunger. It was warmth, fuel, success, maybe life itself.

Our last afternoon was spent in a leisurely way looking the town over. Louis Lebourdais, the telegraph operator, told us that the bridge over the Fraser River, which we would cross on our departure, was built in 1925 and that before that a twin-hulled scow had been used, carried by a cable and propelled across the river by the current, like the one far up the river at McBride. Before that, people had been ferried by river steamers or canoe, and livestock were driven into the water to swim as best they could.

There was still placer gold in both the Fraser and the Quesnel rivers and quite a number of men with gold-pan and rocker were making five dollars a day. For the few jobs that did come up, wages were only two dollars a day.

Ready for the last stretch to Bella Coola, a smiling Ruth and Cliff prepare to leave Quesnel on September 16, 1933.

Next morning, September 16, we clomped across the bridge to the community of West Quesnel, and rode through a collection of small houses occupied by an assortment of "Orientals, Occidentals and accidentals" whose progeny peered from every door and window. Then for a few miles we rode between farmsteads ranging from time-battered, weather-beaten old ones tottering empty-eyed to the ground, to an occasional hopeful new one. We climbed steadily up what people had referred to as a mountain, leaving the little farms behind. Except for the road, we were in the wilderness.

This area had not always been so quiet. In 1866 crews of the Collins Overland Telegraph, aiming at crossing the Bering Straits to Russia, were clearing right-of-way and stringing wire. Through here in 1898 thousands of men stormed on their way to the Yukon. Ashcroft was their rail terminal, Quesnel the place to cross the Fraser. In that year 1,500 men and 3,000 horses left Ashcroft for the Yukon and of these, only six men and no horses reached their destination.

Again in '98, three outfits attempted to drive cattle passing through to the Yukon, competing for first place on the trail, in order to get the best grass. None got their cattle through "on the hoof," but some were slaughtered and delivered by scow. Norman Lee, from the nearby Chilcotin country, lost his 200 head of cattle and arrived back in Vancouver with "a dollar, a dog and a blanket" — and obviously a sense of humour.

In 1910 the government built a wagon road from Blackwater Crossing to Fort George to facilitate mail and passenger delivery to the northern community during the winter when boats could not operate on the Fraser. Stables and office buildings and accommodations for travellers were built, first in West Quesnel and then along the route.

We didn't see a vehicle all day. In camp that night a range bull frightened our horses but went on his way without troubling us. Heavy rain came down, but our little stove, belching with pitchy wood, converted our tent into a luxury apartment, enriched by solitude.

A few days out of Quesnel, it was evident that we were riding into an entirely new world. We climbed the "mountain" and dropped into a great flat basin that stretched over the horizon to the south and north, and to eternity westward. Out of the west the Blackwater River flowed for 150 miles, over a few rapids and falls, through a thousand lakes and twice as many swamps. Sharing this basin with the shining lakes were great dark forests of pine and meadows of deep, waving grass. In its flatness the country contrasted sharply with the Rockies or Cariboo, and was an easy one in which to travel and, by the same token, to get lost.

The lakes in particular were beautiful. Most of them came right to the edge of the forest, and most of them were fringed with

Clouds lie in the water as a northern interior lake mirrors the surrounding scenery.

deciduous trees that at this time of the year were bright yellow and red, all doubled by their reflection in the lake. There were times when fog lifting off a lake made it impossible to tell whether the fleet of islands reflected in the water had surfaced from below or dropped from the clouds above.

Indians, we found, greatly outnumbered white men in the eastern part of this basin and composed its entire population in the western half.

Here, in addition to English, sometimes instead of it, the people spoke in the Chinook jargon of the fur-trade days, which bridged all language gaps. We had learned in Quesnel that an Indian village was a "rancheree," a deer was a "mowitch," an Indian woman was a "klootch" and talk was "wawa." There have been English–Chinook dictionaries printed, and in Kamloops, Father Lejeune published a newspaper in Chinook, the *Kamloops Wawa*, for three decades. Although there are probably less than 300 words in the jargon, each word, as in English, has several different meanings. Combinations are almost infinite in number, and meanings are often arrived at by implication rather than a direct word. A pistol, for instance, is a "tenas (little) musket" and flattery or cajolery is sweet talk or "sugar wawa" or maybe even "honey wawa."

"Kah mika klatawa?" a stranger asked on meeting us, and we could not answer until his companion, a small boy, interpreted "Where are you going?"

Then there was the Indian tongue itself, the Carrier tongue, a soft language of vowels and 't's and 'z's, with the sound of running water and the wind soughing through the lodgepole pines, a true language of the kla-hannie (outdoors). Some of it had got onto maps and such delightful mouthfuls as Tahuntesko Lake, Punkutlaenkut Lakes and Taiateaze River were frequently mulled over.

The fourth day out from Quesnel was one of heavy cold winds that drove us to wear almost all the clothes we had, and then to walk most of the time to keep warm. After hours of walking and riding through burned timber and along windswept ridges, we found good grass and a protected campsite by good water, and though it was only 2:30, we stopped and made a comfortable camp. A comfortable camp, in our language, only exceeded the ordinary camp in that we cut three or four armloads of spruce boughs and by laying the butts to the ground, arranged them as feathers to make a bed as soft as ever a mattress manufacturer dreamed, and as aromatic as a young forest itself. In an ordinary camp our mattress was made of the saddle blankets, carefully laid "horse-side" down, covered with a layer or two of canvas to contain horse-smell, and then our bedding. In a comfortable camp the tent walls were so firmly weighted with rocks, and pegged down, that mice would be unable to intrude; a rope was strung just under the peak of the tent for a clothes or towel-drying rack — and most essential, an hour or two of leisure, after camp chores, to enjoy it.

For even the ordinary camp, our routine was to unpack the horses, leave the saddles on, get the tent up and packs inside, get the stove up and fire going — all of which took about half an hour. Then as Ruth prepared supper, I looked after the horses, cut enough wood for the night and piled it inside the tent by the stove. (We carried dry kindling each day to the next camp to assure a quick fire.) Canvas pack-covers made a complete floor covering, pack boxes a table and pile of saddles in a corner something to lean against. Thus was our home made each night and our gear protected. In these surroundings, lighted by the warm orange glow of a candle or two, we shed the fatigue of the trail and prepared for the morrow.

About 4:30 that afternoon a team and wagon came in from the west and a lone man unhitched the horses and tied them to the wagon. Presently the smoke from his campfire spread through the trees and I went over to visit him. A small tent had been erected in a dry wash a few yards from the wagon and a fire started on a small pile of logs. He had been reading, and as I approached, he put down his book.

He was John Ward, Paul Krestinuk's partner, in from Algatchuz. He was glad of the visit, hadn't seen a white face in a month. He had two Indians with him, driving a small herd of cattle, and he would be sharing this camp with them. No, all three didn't sleep in that tent. The other two wrapped themselves in a piece of canvas and slept under a tree.

Just then a rider came up: a dark, well-built Indian who dismounted, and with a handy butcher knife, cut two ribs from a moose rack that was in the wagon, impaled them on a stick and held them in the flames until the meat was black and smoking. Whereupon he attacked it with strong teeth, occasionally wiping the grease from his lips and chin with a piece of bread, which he then ate. This process complete, he threw the bare bones into the fire, wiped his fingers on his buckskin chaps, leaped on his horse and galloped away.

The book that trader Ward had laid down, I noted, was the complete works of William Shakespeare.

"You are a student of Shakespeare?" I asked.

Ward rejected the idea. "No, but I like my reading as far removed from this country as I can get it. It's a relief from roots and windfall and Jack-pine jungles."

Ruth called, and with Ward's promise that if I returned in the morning he would give me some data about Indian life in this country, I went to our tent, and we, too, shut out memories of unpleasant surroundings.

Next morning I went over again. John enjoyed an attentive audience and launched immediately into his story. His Indian henchmen had gone, the camp dismantled.

"Not many years ago," he began, "one of the prettiest girls of the tribe ... no, she was the prettiest ... got thrown from a horse and must have got hurt, because she had a pain in her side ever after. Her father was a tribal medicine man and he tried to cure her, but failed. He called in three or four of the other medicine men and they failed, too. The girl died.

"I tried to get the police to come out and investigate the matter, but they said it was too far. I think they didn't want to ride that far on a horse.

"I wrote an account of it for the *Observer* in Quesnel, and when it was published, the priest got into hot water from his superiors

137

for allowing such things to go on, so there was a black eye for everyone concerned.

"The Indian doctor's way of treatment is to dance around for a great deal, chanting and shouting and leaping, warm his hands over the stove, rub the patient's sore spots for a moment, then scrape the affected parts with cupped hands and blow the pain into the air, declaring it to be gone. It's just hypnotism and that's all! Sometimes it works. This time it didn't.

"The Indians didn't like the stir I created, the priest got mad, and now the Indians won't let me look in on such things."

I helped him harness his horses, (they ate from the wagon load of hay, so there was no wandering horse problems here) hitched up for him and bade him goodbye.

We made our own start about 11:15, climbed over the summit of the hill we had been ascending all the way from Quesnel, then made a long descent, crossed the Nazko River on a bridge and rode north through the Nazko "Rancheree." It was a collection of old cabins, with several tents added, in the doorways of which two Indian mothers suckled their young and older children peeped shyly. The white-painted frame chapel looked over the village, the graveyard with its numerous crosses, the trading post and the dogs that ran out to bark at us. No men seemed present.

Next day we crossed the Blackwater River, a clear stream flowing over a bed of black rocks that gave it a dark appearance.

This was an exciting moment for us. More than three months ago we had set out to cross the mountain ranges to follow in the footsteps of Alexander Mackenzie to the Pacific Ocean. Here, after a series of trying adventures, during which we discovered that the area west of the Rockies was almost as unknown to us as it had been to the great explorer himself, we were on the same river.

We were to find that the country and conditions had changed little in the many-score years that had elapsed. There were now permanent Indian villages of log and sometimes frame structure, with the ever-present church rising above, where before there had been Kekuli holes for the winter and portable shelters of skins during the summer. The trails had been widened to accommodate horses and packs, sleighs and even wagons, and the ruts had been made deeper, for steel horseshoes cut deeper than moccasins. But, we were to learn, one could travel for a week on end and not see a white man, and the Indians still looked to the forests and streams for their livelihood.

We wondered when these people first got horses. Mackenzie had seen none in 1793, but Fraser had noted that the Indians around Lillooet were skilled horsemen in 1808, while still farther south the Lewis and Clark expedition in 1825 considered the Indians' possession of horses as only to be expected.

Mackenzie had started from his wintering post on the Peace River east of the Rockies in May of 1793 with nine companions, a dog and 3,000 pounds of trade goods and baggage in a paper-thin canoe. Fighting their way up the frightening spring freshet on the Peace River, they found the Parsnip almost as difficult. A portage took them to a stream flowing into the Fraser River, through swamp and fallen timber and over cascades that smashed their canoe, robbed them of much of their supplies and continually threatened them with destruction. Their guide deserted them. But eventually they embarked on the broad Fraser River and floated in the direction they wished to go. East of the Rockies Mackenzie had been told of two big rivers flowing into the Pacific Ocean but he had failed to recognize there was more than one. The mouth of the Columbia had been discovered by Robert Grey in 1792, but Mackenzie could not have learned of it, and the Fraser's mouth had not yet been detected. He called the great river now bearing him the Tacouche Tesse.

Downstream, the Natives convinced him that if he were to continue along the river he would meet with murderous rapids and warlike Indians. If he wanted to reach the Stinking Lake (the Indians' name for the ocean) a grand traverse would take them along a well-marked trading path through the towering mountains to a short river that flowed into the sea. The journey would take four days some said, maybe six, maybe eight. Mackenzie, worried about diminishing supplies and about getting back over the Rockies before unpredictable winter weather barred the way, decided to stake all on an overland dash to the Pacific.

Turning upstream at the point later to be called Alexandria, he found the mouth of the river he called Westroad. Here he cached the canoe, buried some gunpowder, pemmican and wild rice against their return and started on the long hike. His men were loaded with 90-pound packs plus their muskets and personal effects, and he carried a similar weight but bore survey instruments instead of a gun.

The trail was well marked and many people were travelling on it. Some had metal trade goods secured from coastal people, and there were even several people from the Pacific shore. This trail they were following was one of the "grease trails," so called because of the large volumes of fish oil from the coast that were traded over it.

The most highly prized of these oils, eulachon grease, was used by the Natives not only as food, but also as a skin dressing and hair tonic. Mackenzie, attempting to keep his guides from deserting, kept guard over them by sleeping with them, not always a pleasure because of the vermin in their garments and the rancid fish oil in their hair.

Our guide, the trader's wagon road, never tried desertion, but more recently used branch roads occasionally led us to hay meadows or fish camps, causing us to lose a half-day's travel at times. It was quite a relief when on the second morning out from Nazko, we rode into another Indian village.

We stopped in front of the row of four houses from beneath which a dozen dogs rushed out, barking loudly. One of the houses was decorated with shooting star decorations on the ridge and along the edge of the roof and as we watched, a door opened and a lean old man emerged. He was so brown as to be almost black, with white hair and startlingly prominent whites to his eyes. He stared at us fixedly, seemingly alarmed as he approached.

Eulachon grease was the most highly prized of fish oils traded over the "grease trail." Aboriginal people used it not only as food, but also as a skin dressing and hair tonic.

"Is this the road to Algatcho?" I asked. At the sound of my voice he stopped short, blinked his eyes but said nothing.

"Do you know Paul Krestinuk?" I tried again, with the same result.

"Parlez-vous Français?" I tried again with one of the few French phrases I remembered from school.

His agitation became worse and he called wildly to someone in the house.

"Oh, you've frightened him," said Ruth, and I couldn't tell whether her voice carried alarm or amusement, for at that moment a door opened and a young man stepped out.

The two exchanged brief messages, then the old fellow, eyes averted, returned to his house. The other turned to us with a smile.

"You will have to excuse the old man," he said in amazingly good English, "he thought you were someone who was killed in an accident a couple of years ago and had come back to life."

Yes, this was the Algatcho road. Just keep on over a little hill. There are some forks in the road, so take the first left fork, then the right one the second time and the left one the third time.

"I'll get a horse and show you," he offered.

We demurred. We could follow the road from his directions, and we didn't want him to go to that trouble. We dared not explain that with only 65 cents left between us, we could not pay for special services.

"I'll catch up to you then," he promised. "I have to go there anyway."

Fifteen minutes later, astride a capable short-coupled mount, he overtook us. He was wearing a beautifully beaded fringed buckskin jacket and flaring batwing chaps made of thick moosehide.

"Wild leather is cheaper and easier to come by in this country than cloth," he said in reply to my compliments on his garb. "Our meat comes wrapped in it."

His village was the Trout Lake Rancheree and he was Johnny Slash. The old man I had alarmed by being alive was Trout Lake Johnny.

Trout Lake was 26 miles from Nazko, a reasonable day's journey by wagon or sleigh, and although called a village was the dwelling place of only several generations of one family. In fact, Johnny Slash was a foundling, picked up by the older man out of a camp otherwise totally destroyed by smallpox around the turn of the century. He, Johnny the younger, had been quite a bit with whites in his boyhood, could read and write a little and knew about Alexander Mackenzie.

"He camped about nine miles west of here at what we call Dry Lake. He stayed for three days. The Indians then were superstitious and wouldn't touch any food scraps or anything else the white men had thrown out. The mother of the old man you saw back there was about 10 years old at the time and she spied on the white men. She died about 20 years ago."

We wondered if this could be accurate. If she had been 10 years old in 1793 and lived until 20 years ago — 1913 — she was 130 years old at the time of her death. Mackenzie's diary contained no mention of a three-day stopover.

"We had tough luck last year," Johnny told us as we rode the length of the longest meadow we had ever seen since the prairies, "there wasn't much moisture during the summer so we didn't get much hay. Then in the winter we got lots of rain and it coated all the meadows with ice and the cattle and horses couldn't rustle. We ran out of hay and lost most of our stock."

With some final words of advice on how to recognize the Dry Lake campsite, Johnny wished us well and departed on his own business. A good man, that Trout Lake man, as interested in learning about his fellow travellers as we were about him, or as Mackenzie was 140 years ago.

There were far more people living along the Blackwater River in 1793 than there were now. Mackenzie had met groups of people every hour or two, but we travelled for days on end without seeing anyone. A smallpox epidemic and the continuing scourge of tuberculosis probably accounted for the decrease in population.

When Johnny Slash left us, we rode through open forest, along limpid streams, past mirror-like lakes, and waded across meadows knee-deep in grass. At least half a dozen perfect campsites were discovered and passed up. Ducks rose from the streams, and, from the lakes, geese clanged their way skyward or watched us pass with varying degrees of caution. If we remained on our horses they were not frightened but if we dismounted the alarm was sounded immediately. Half a dozen deer in as many miles bounded away, and from opposite sides of a little lake two moose paced into the forest.

A spot between lakes, with tent poles leaning into trees, picket pegs in the meadows and bark stripped off the pine trees was the Dry Lake campsite. There was no "dry" lake, but that would have been impossible following all the rain that had fallen.

Across one of the lakes on a bit of beach not a hundred yards distant, two coyotes frolicked as we approached, then watched us erect camp. As we set up our "comfortable camp" — we had decided to stay over and rest the horses — geese and ducks flew continuously from one lake to another. We were, according to Johnny Slash's figures, 115 miles out of Quesnel.

We were very pleased with our progress. Mackenzie would have been disgusted. He had taken only four days to come from the Fraser. It had taken us seven. He and his men carried close to a hundred pounds each on their backs and travelled from 4:30 or 5:00 in the morning until sometimes 9:00 at night. A 7:00 a.m. start called for an apology, while if he wished to "indulge" his men, he postponed departure time until 9:00 in the morning. In contrast, we were happy with a start before 10:00, and we hoped to be in our next camp by 4:00 in the afternoon. When we chose to indulge our horses, we gave them a whole day's rest.

The wildlife would not permit us to sleep late the following morning. Except for the continual whistle of ducks flying overhead, which was in itself surprising, the night was peaceful enough until the first hint of coming day outlined trees against the sky, when a choir of coyotes began running up and down the scales and rising into lyrical laughing ecstasies. This continued until a wolf howl stopped it. There was a short silence and then a thousand waterfowl began to chatter, day was officially born, and further sleep was impossible.

After breakfast I went out with the revolver (our only weapon) to try and bag a fowl but got nothing more than powder smoke in my eyes. The heavy back and wing feathers of sitting geese and ducks are effective armour against a .22 bullet and no one but a movie hero would attempt to bring a goose or duck out of the air with such a small weapon. I was almost relieved when a snowstorm with dime-sized flakes drove me back to camp. After all, grouse were abundant, tasty and vulnerable.

The snowstorm dumped about two inches on the ground, then the weather cleared enough to melt most of it by late afternoon.

As Ruth was getting supper, I went to bring the horses in closer to camp. I had heard their bells and knew their approximate location, so I had no difficulty finding them, but as I approached them, they "spooked," a most unusual thing for them to do, and it took me another 15 minutes to get ahead of them and turn them toward what I thought was the direction of camp. It seemed to take longer than I thought it should, and I was relieved when we came to the shore of a lake. Our camp was on a lake and in a few minutes we would be there. But my relief was short-lived, for presently I could see an island in the lake, a distinctive rock island that I had certainly never seen before. In another quarter of a mile a second rocky island appeared, and I tasted a strong sip of fear. It was beginning to get dark, I had no coat and I did not know where our camp was.

Determinedly fighting down panic, I got ahead of the horses again and turned them about. But with two of them hobbled, they travelled slowly — there was about 15 minutes of visibility left — so I left them and followed our tracks back. This was not difficult as the hobbled horses had dug little gouges in the earth, and there was an occasional patch of snow where tracks showed plainly. As I backtracked I shouted frequently and shot the revolver, but both sounded feeble.

Then I heard an answering call and saw Ruth ahead of me standing on a little hill, and behind her, the tent was a faint orange wedge in the gathering darkness.

We discussed the escapade over the evening meal. Ruth was a good cook, but never on any other mountain trip had I fared as well.

I was embarrassed and concerned by the thoughts of what might have happened if she had been left alone in the wilderness miles from civilization.

"What would you have done?" I asked.

"I didn't have to find out, did I?" she replied simply. "I won't have to find out."

The discussion ended there. I felt that it was a good lesson, almost painlessly administered.

145

Next morning when I went for the horses, the tracks showed I had been driving them directly away from camp. They were hard to find and hard to catch. We wondered if it paid to "indulge" them.

We had been on the trail several hours when the smell of wood smoke alerted us to the presence of others, and in a few minutes we came upon an Indian camp of three tents set around a fire under long racks loaded with dark red meat. There were numerous horses, fat and sleek-looking, tied to trees and a number of dogs, equally well fed. They didn't bother to raise the alarm at our approach. There were three women, two almost fully grown boys and a big, handsome man. Children darted in and out of the tents so fast that it was impossible to guess their number.

The man greeted us with friendly gusto and we inquired about the trail.

"You're on it," he replied, "all same cattle trail all the way to Algatcho."

The meat on the racks interested us.

"Moose," he said. "We shot two, right close here and brought the women out to dry the meat. You want some?"

Natives dry strips of meat on racks over a slow fire — the same method used for drying fish.

But grouse had fallen to our little revolver and we didn't think we could carry the moose meat without spoiling it.

"Do you know pemmican?" I asked, and when he looked puzzled I added, "That's the Hudson's Bay Company way of keeping meat for the trail."

He laughed.

"I thought maybe it was a man's name. We do it always like this, same as fish, cut in strips and smoked and dried over a slow fire. It will last for years if you keep it dry … and don't eat it."

Moose had not been known in this area for long, we were to learn, indeed not much before the turn of the century. In the Chilcotin country, 50 or 60 miles to the south of us, the first moose was sighted about 1905 by an Indian who, getting a sight of the huge palmated antlers, went terrified to the priest with the story he had surely seen the devil himself, For a while, although they shot them, the Indians refused to eat the meat. In the Trout Lake reserve the meat was refused as late as 1910. The moose migration from the north was triggered by extensive deciduous growth, which sprang up in the wake of the forest fires attending settlement. Caribou almost disappeared from the range, creating the belief that the moose drove them out. Another theory suggested that the fires burned the "caribou moss" on which they fed.

The moose we saw were legion, the caribou none.

When we asked if we could take pictures, the number of children they hauled from the tents were also legion.

That night all the water in our tent froze solid. Next day we walked most of the time to keep warm, even though the sun shone brightly. When it started to snow as we packed the following morning, we got the underlined, emphasized message that winter was coming to this country and we should be getting out of it. The date was September 26.

Later, we were puzzling over which fork in the road to take when a young Indian on a splendid black mount rode up from behind.

"You come this way," he said. "It short way."

He knew about our travels because he had visited at the hunter's camp. The big man, he said, was Chief Mollis but when he referred to his horse as a fast "lunna" and that he had caught a "led" fox we asked him if the man was really Chief Morris.

"Yes. That's him. Chief Mollis of Kluskus Lake Lanchellee!"

Our erstwhile guide stopped at his own cabin and we rode on for several hours, had a bite of lunch and came to the Kluskus Lakes and the Indian settlement there.

At first we thought it was a deserted village, for nothing moved, not even dogs, until we saw an old Indian woman seated beside a pile of tanned moosehide. She was working, braiding long strips of hide into rope. She said her man was out hunting, that she was entirely alone in the village. When I asked to take her picture in her house, she giggled agreement, and, with her finger in her mouth, went in and sat down by some moccasins on which she was putting the finishing trim. The house was spotlessly clean, with table covered with bright oilcloth, and some chairs. A large collapsible tin stove perched on a pile of rocks and a mahogany mantel clock ticked on a shelf held by two wooden pegs driven into the wall.

Close to a crucifix hung a large photograph of three children.

"Yours?" I asked.

"Yes," she replied quietly, "but all dead now. They get bad coughing sickness."

We asked if she had meat, and when she shook her head we gave her two grouse, which seemed to surprise her. It undoubtedly pleased her, for goodbye was an invitation to come back again.

The graveyard on top of a hill overlooking the lake seemed well populated, and the little grave-houses and fences around the graves were in many cases neatly painted.

These people were the Carriers, described by Father Morice in his 1904 book *The History of the Northern Interior of British Columbia*, in which he states: "The Carriers, who have villages all the way from Stuart Lake and tributaries to Alexandria on the Fraser … are stouter and more heavily built, with coarser traits, thicker lips (than the more northerly Sekanais on the west slope of the Rockies) and quite large eyes." And ... "in the case of death the bodies were buried among the Chilcotins and Shuswaps, burned among the Carriers ...

"Among the Carriers, the widow of a deceased warrior used to pick up from the ashes of the funeral pyre the few charred bones

An old woman of the Carriers stands beside her tent under a spruce-bark shelter at a fish camp.

149

which escaped the fire and carry them on her back in a little leathern satchel — hence the name of the tribe — until the co-clansmen of the deceased had amassed a sufficient quantity of eatables and dressed skins to be publicly distributed among people of different clans, in the course of an ostentatious ceremony called 'potlatch,' a ceremony which prevailed among all the Sekanais and the eastern Nahanais tribes."

The term Carriers could well be applied to them for another reason, that they were carriers of merchandise along this grease trail between the peoples of the coast and those of the Upper Fraser valley.

Coastal peoples have simplified it by calling them "Stick Indians" or "Sticks" because the trees surrounding them are small compared with the towering ones around coastal villages.

Our Kluskus Lake camp that evening was on the edge of a living picture created by the Master Painter. Across the water white clouds billowed up into a city of castles brushed deep with purple shadows. Mirrored in the lake a similar city was inverted, and separated from its ethereal original by a band of yellow poplars and scarlet willows. A loon's lonesome call winged into the distance and night rose silently out of the shadows to bestow peace upon the world while two minute humans, eating their supper, sat with tent flaps open and watched the light fade from the living canvas.

The cheerless miles of burned timber next day terminated in mid-afternoon with a big meadow of excellent grass and we accepted the unspoken invitation. We put our tent among some young poplars at the edge of the meadow from which we could see rising, just beyond the hills at the other end of the meadow, a huge snow-clad triangular peak. Its snowy sides showed that winter was already there and its shape prompted the nickname "Old Fujiyama."

Our stopover here was marked by wind that came with morning light, and blew from the mountain down the meadow for almost the whole of the day, threatening to uproot our tent. We could have moved into a deep, damp, dark spruce thicket, but instead spent hours anchoring the tent with boulders and cutting and dragging into place a dozen young conifers for a windbreak. We let the fire die down in the little stove lest this should cause trouble, and when the wind did abate in late afternoon the relief was as if a physical weight had been lifted.

This site was also the scene of what could have been disaster or death from a wild animal. Our horses were tied to trees near camp, the tent was packed and we were ready to start saddling when from up the meadow came the sound of a repeated coughing bellow, and we saw a huge black bull moose with antlers like a hayrack come pacing toward us, his head low and swinging from side to side as he bellowed. Many woodsmen are convinced that a bull moose is the most dangerous animal in the woods, and this huge specimen, at the height of the rutting season, seemed to be in a pugnacious mood.

Our sole weapon, the revolver, ineffective against geese or even ducks, certainly had no place in this picture!

"What will we do if he comes near camp?" Ruth asked.

"Get behind a tree and stand perfectly still," I suggested, for want of anything better to say.

Thus a tableau rapidly developed, featuring a mighty moose standing within 50 feet of a partially dismantled camp, a young man and woman standing statue-like behind trees, 20 feet away from each other, and beyond them, perhaps a hundred feet from the moose, four horses also standing like graven images, waiting. Everything waited.

The bull stopped bellowing as if he had detected something unusual. Lifting his head, he moved it slowly from side to side, studying the situation. I could see him swallow. Turning my eyes only, I looked at Ruth to see how she was faring under the tension, and as I did so she looked back at me. The horses, watching the moose, didn't make a sound. For a full two minutes there were seven still-life statues on the edge of that northern meadow. Only eyes moved.

Then the moose decided he had business in another quarter, for he turned, circled our camp and disappeared among some willows and we saw no more of him.

151

As we packed we had a strong feeling that Somebody up there loved us!

It was another day of wind, rain, mud and Jack pine. We began to think we were approaching Algatchuz, and were looking for it around every corner when we met a young man on a sweaty, impatient horse.

How far was it to Algatcho? (We decided on the phonetic pronunciation because that was the way everyone said it.)

"Pipty miles, mabe," the man replied.

"Fifty miles," I echoed in disappointment. That would take us another three days. "It can't be that far!"

"Look my horse," the man said, "I come since daylight. Plitty fast." The sweat and lather testified the horse had been moving.

We exchanged names. His was Lassees West. West was a good name. We wondered if Lassees was the result of any transposition of letters, but could think of none.

An hour or so later we crossed the Blackwater on a bridge (we had already crossed it once from north to south on an easy knee-deep ford) built by the energetic Paul Krestinuk, and on a tree beside the bridge a sign stated simply: ALGATCHO 45 MILES.

Next day at the establishment of one Alexis (Blackwater Alexis to distinguish him from a score of other Alexises) we asked a group of two young men and an older woman how far it was to Algatcho, and received three different answers, "pipteen" miles, 18 miles and 25 miles. When we finally did get there, we would have said 30 miles. So much for elastic miles.

It snowed that night, the third time since leaving Quesnel, and the horses pawed for grass. We were concerned lest the snow be deep enough to hide the wagon tracks we were following, which would cause us needless deviations, particularly in burns or meadows. But as we packed, a heavy, warm rain started, which reduced the snow to slush and before noon had washed it all away. Then it turned cold again and we walked to avoid being frozen into blocks of ice.

It seemed to us that day that Algatcho, capital city of the Carriers, became a living creature receding as we advanced. The double-tracked trail, our only assurance that people had passed this way before, led us past several small lakes, one being Ulgack Lake, the ultimate source of the Blackwater River. It sloshed us through endless miles of dark Jack pine, slogging through mud, stumbling over boulders, and along a ridge where the wind drove the rain horizontally into our faces and found entry in openings around our necks and wrists. As the afternoon wore on we hoped for, prayed for, then despaired of finding a campsite for the night.

Then through the trees we came upon a collection of little grey houses. Algatcho! Grey houses they were indeed, darker on the north and west sides because of the driving rain — grey houses merging with a forest of crosses and grave-houses, seeking shelter under a great unpainted crazily leaning church holding a cross high against the scurrying clouds.

But there were no people. No dogs rushed out at us. No smoke rose from the tin chimneys. No lights glowed in the little windows and no men stepped out from opening doors. As we rode down the main street we called frequently. There were no answering echoes.

The village was on a little hill above a lake, toward which a well-beaten path led. It was a route, if such stories were true, over which Indian brides hauled water with vigour to illustrate what a fine wife her husband had got. To the left there seemed to be room for a meadow and I was wondering which of a half-dozen trails into the intervening stretch of wood led there when my mount stopped with a snort. His actions bespoke a bear at close quarters, but when I followed his pointing ears there was, not a bear, but an old Indian woman.

She hadn't been there seconds before. My horse's actions testified to that. Half-believing she might be a materialization of one of the cloud wraiths swirling around the treetops, I attempted conversation with her.

"Hello. Are you the only one here?"

No answer.

"Are the men all out hunting?"

Still no answer.

"Maybe she's deaf," Ruth suggested.

"Bella Coola," I shouted, acting on Ruth's idea, "which way is Bella Coola?"

The woman's arm rose, made a complete circle, then dropped again to her side.

"There you are," Ruth said. "Just out there."

"Horse feed," I shouted. "Grass. Pasture. Meadow."

One of the words must have carried the message. Wordlessly she turned and started down a forest path, and we followed closely lest she vaporize and disappear.

Shortly we emerged from the forest on to a meadow that dipped into the lake.

The old woman stood silently as we assessed the situation. I untied a grouse from my saddle and gave it to her with shouted thanks. Then she silently floated, moccasin-quiet, back down the trail.

"At least she walked away," I said, watching her for a moment before jumping to the task of unpacking and setting up camp as the shadows flowed out of the woods and flooded the meadow and lake.

We had set Algatcho as our goal where we would get a guide to show us to the Dean and its doubtful crossing. Could that old lady act as a guide?

The wind had died at dusk, and through the night, the clouds parted sufficiently to permit periods of bright moonlight, but by our calculations the moon was directly north of us.

Out on the lake, loons called.

"Could that be the Indian woman talking to her neighbours?" I asked.

"I think it is time we had a good sleep," was Ruth's reply, and, suiting action to word, slept soundly until morning.

Next morning the sun shone. The horses, leaving good grass, were plugged in fallen timber above the lake, their discovery and extrication delaying our departure until 11:00 a.m.

This time our tour of the village was even less rewarding than that of the evening before, producing no old Indian lady, nor anyone else. No smoke rose from any chimney, and all the windows were dark and blank. The sun, perceptibly lower in the southeastern sky, for this was the second of October, picked out the distressing loneliness of the place, casting long shadows from the strange decorations on the grave-houses, glinting a winking light from one granite tombstone. From the peak of one grave-house a crow cawed cheerlessly. But again, no people.

Sitting our horses on the little hill, we could see to the west and southwest a range of high, sharp snowy peaks, the Coast Range. Between it and us a great basin of timber fell, to rise again and be lost in the snows of the mountains. Down there, in that basin, the Dean River flowed across our path.

We had hoped to find a guide at Algatcho to show us across the Dean. Somewhere in one of those houses was the little old lady. Were there others silently watching us?

"Let's get out of here before we go crazy," urged Ruth.

The sun had given us direction and when we found a trail leading towards the Dean we followed it past small lakes, down a wide avenue chopped as for a highway or railway, down some squishy meadows and through burnt forest to a big meadow with some haystacks and an obvious Indian encampment beside a big clear stream flowing from the southeast.

It must be the Dean!

The dubious, dangerous, deadly Dean!

Krestinuk had warned us against it. Ward had repeated the warning. Away back in the prairies, classroom history books had stated that Mackenzie had "succeeded in crossing the Dean River on a raft," intimating danger, thrill and accomplishment.

The campsite, ideally set among some trees the Indian way to gain their protection and warmth (rather than coldly out on grassy meadows like a farmhouse on a prairie field as with most white-man camps), invited us to postpone the crossing until the morrow, to dry our gear and rest. We accepted.

At this camp, besides a birchbark berry pail and a pair of very junior moccasins that had been hung on a limb to dry and then forgotten, we found a message written on a piece of cardboard in the Cree alphabet that missionary James Evans at distant Norway House had developed almost a hundred years ago. This art had been transposed, adapted to the Carrier language by that zealous priest, Father Morice, and introduced into New Caledonia in the form of printed news-sheets.

That afternoon we ruminated over all the bad things that had been said of the Dean River crossing, and of the trail over the mountains. We had been told that from Anahim Lake, 40 or 50 miles up the Dean River, a telegraph line accompanied by a "telegraph trail" followed a much less hazardous route to Bella Coola. In fact this telegraph trail was the winter path, used when the other, called also a "summer trail," couldn't be used. Our map showed a trail going up the east side, our side of the Dean, so we decided to take the longer Anahim Lake route.

But three hours of hard bushwhacking and swamp-floundering next day proved our map to be, once more, a work of fiction. There was no trail along the east side of the Dean. We returned to our camp, and decided to try the crossing next morning when the horses were rested. As Ruth said, we would still be on Mackenzie's trail, which is what we set out to follow.

Packs next morning were placed high, clothes wrapped in canvas, all set for a swimming crossing.

"When I'm across," I said to Ruth, "put the packhorses in. And if they make it, you come."

I rode into the water, feet free of the stirrups, studying the river in front of the horse's feet, alert for traps. But there weren't any. The bottom was of small round pebbles, the water not to the horse's knees. In three minutes I was on the far side and the rest were splashing happily to join me.

We had been misled by a monstrous myth. Unless the Indians had supplied Mackenzie with ready-made rafts, he wasted a lot of time making them, rather than have his men wade the river as any 10-year-old boy could have done.

Sir Alexander Mackenzie crossed the Dean River in 1793 at this same spot. Ruth and Cliff and their horses are able to ford the river easily, proving wrong the myth that a raft was necessary to cross it.

Having laid that bogey to rest, and the sun still blessing us with dry warmth, we proceeded westward along a chain of lakes and meadows. That evening we camped in a little protected pocket, and led the horses a quarter of a mile along the trail to good grass. Next morning when we went to get them their tracks had been entirely obliterated by multiple bear tracks, and judging by the claw marks of the front pads, some impressive grizzlies. If they had inspected our camp in the night they left no evidence.

We were several hours on the trail when we met a young Indian and his wife with six head of packhorses. They were driving them, and as we stopped to talk, the packhorses kept on travelling as if they were on their way home.

Yes, this was the Bella Coola trail. This couple had been to Bella Coola. All the people of Algatcho had been there. The rest of the Algatcho people were about a day's journey behind, and we would meet them all travelling together. The brother of this young man had died in Bella Coola at the hospital and they had brought his body up from the valley floor onto a bench, and had buried him alongside the trail.

The couple had camped twice since leaving the Bella Coola Valley. We were glad to hear that. We thought our speed would equal theirs.

Two hours after saying goodbye to them we came upon their camp. A couple of logs were still smoking, and as we piled earth on them, we blamed such neglected campfires for the forests of dead grey spars between here and Quesnel. They had tied their horses to trees for the night to save themselves the trouble of collecting them in the morning, a practice only permissible on very short trips indeed.

That afternoon we came to an extensive fish-drying shed, 50 or 60 feet long at the outlet of Squiness Fish Lake. The place was deserted, because it was late in the season, but it was evidence that the Natives still depended very largely on fish for their food.

We passed up a beautiful campsite, forded a river about a quarter the size of the Dean and then refused an even more attractive site. We crawled up a steep hill well barricaded with fallen timber, knit with regrowth and fortified with huge boulders, the steepest going since Barkerville. Then we began to worry lest we have to do as our recent acquaintances did, tie our horses to trees for the night. We were relieved to meet a small pack train with two men who said there was a small meadow about a mile distant.

The mile grew to two or three, and it was dusk when we got there and found the spot more marshy than meadowy. But it was better than the only alternative — nothing — and in an attempt to compensate for its shortcomings, we indulged the horses (would we never learn) by turning them loose without hobble or drag. O'Hara wore the bell.

We did, however, pitch the tent in such a manner along the trail that any back-trailing horse would almost have to trample on it. This stratagem worked once; in about an hour the horses approached the tent with departure in mind and we intercepted them and drove them noisily back to the meadow. But the next time around, O'Hara leading the way with his bell, they took a noisy, brush-crashing detour wide of the tent and went hurrying back along the trail.

We spent the night hoping they would stop at the first meadow, about eight miles distant, and we were astir at four, breakfasted and on the trail before daylight. The horses were not in the first meadow and we had visions of them going on and on. I had never heard of horses completely deserting a party but the story of one overnight wander of 40 miles kept nagging me. We broke ice with a club on the little river between the two meadows and waded knee-deep through it, and three and a half hours after leaving camp we found our horses contentedly lying in the second meadow.

Back at camp, we were packing when a party consisting of two Indian women, each with a baby, two children about 10 years old and two smaller boys riding on a bareback horse, arrived and stopped to talk.

One of the mothers was going to meet her brother at Fish Lake on top of the mountain ahead of us, "maybe tonight, maybe tomorrow." If they did not meet him they would camp, with no gear, overnight.

Our afternoon's travel, predestined to be short, took us on a sharp climb steadily southward, out of the Dean River trough. We were climbing once more into high mountains and west of us, ice falls cascaded down an outstanding lofty peak. Thunder Mountain, 9,000 feet according to our map, was living up to its name.

About four o'clock we came to a dry, hard meadow with the required grass, wood and water so we camped. This time we showed no indulgence to the horses. Each animal was firmly picketed and just in case a picket pulled or a rope broke, a set of bars was put strategically across the trail.

Ice falls sounding like thunder from 10 miles away likely explain how Thunder Mountain in Coast Range got its name.

It froze in earnest through the night, layering the grass with frost and making the picket ropes, which during the day were pack ropes, so stiff you could drive a nail 10 feet away with one. Thunder Mountain continued to boom and a black cloud with no good intent drifted ominously over it.

We had been on the trail half an hour when we came upon the group of Indians, the main population of Algatcho that we had been told to expect. One man with a small rifle over his arm, accompanied by a half-grown boy, had left the main body as if getting the horses packed and on the trail was somebody else's job. The others, about 35 of them, were breaking camp, the men shouting orders and chasing horses, the women busy packing and a child or two wailing in distress at the noise and confusion. We did not add to the turmoil, but pushed on with only an exchange of greetings. We were not yet out of earshot when two horses, each with multiple human burdens, left this melee and overtook us. One carried one of the Indian mothers we had met yesterday, babe on back, and the other was double-decking the two boys, still without a saddle. They were going to Bella Coola.

We welcomed their company. The young woman would be able to supply some local information. Besides, the fact of an Indian mother with a babe in basket and two other small children travelling unescorted over it encouraged us to believe the trail might not be as bad as pictured.

Ever since crossing the Dean River we had been drawing a big half-circle around a range of brightly coloured extinct volcanoes. They had been south of us, now they were east, their tops covered with snow, their sides showing streaks of red, yellow, purple and brown. Instead of skirting them as we were doing, Mackenzie had gone through the range, up a valley that produced some marmots, a small deer and some horrible weather. The Indian woman only giggled when I asked her about "the first white man to come through here." "Didn't know him," she said, but she did say the mountains "over there" to our left were "the mountains that bleed."

"Do Indian people still eat marmots?" I asked.

"Oh, yes," she said. "Delate kloshe muck-a-muck (very good food)" and laughed, maybe at her Chinook, maybe at me for asking so many questions.

At the top of the range where he began his descent into Bella Coola Valley, the explorer stated, "It now began to hail, rain and snow, nor could we find any shelter but the leewardside of a huge rock. The wind also rose into a tempest and the weather was as distressing as any I had ever experienced."

He suggested they leave half the deer in the snow at the top of the pass, but his men insisted they take it all with them, and, when they reached timber, they made a heartier meal than they had for many a day.

Here also he observed a "stupendous mountain whose snow-clad summit was lost in the clouds." On our map of the region we saw a MOUNT STUPENDOUS marked, bordering the south side of the valley opposite the awesome defile down which Mackenzie plunged to the Bella Coola River.

On the horse trail that succeeded the original "grease trail" we climbed steadily into altitudes where the trees were stunted and clung in tight little clumps to protect themselves from the killer winds and frosts in this terrain. Rocky shoulders lifting out of the slopes had epaulets of gaunt tree skeletons, their foliage and lesser branches long torn off, the supporters around their feet destroyed and lifting bare grey limbs against the advancing clouds.

As we climbed, high mountains rose all about us, as if we were crawling onto a stage with huge peaks in the galleries looking down on us. We struggled over the edge of the lofty platform and for a while, we were in an alpine grassland where larch, tamarack and spruce shared the landscape with yellow meadows.

Around us on three sides rose the sharp, ice-festooned peaks of the Coast Range, with clouds spilling over from the west, while northeast of us the blunt Rainbows, "volcanoes-with-their-heads blown off," showed as great long sweeping uplifts of white.

Near a half-frozen lake, surrounded by pockets of meadows between rocky ribs that had been scraped and scoured by ancient ice caps, we stopped for a few minutes to graze the horses. The Indian woman said she was going on.

"You be all right," she said. "Trail all down hill now. You don't get lost."

She trotted away. A wraith-like cloud sweeping across the plateau enveloped her and her children. We never saw them again.

"Hump" Lake, with Mount Stupendous in the background, is a trail-side beauty spot.

Our little parting tableau had been watched, undoubtedly, by a lone figure seated by a small fire on a hummock a hundred yards or so distant. I rode over to talk but as I approached he threw the bone he had been chewing on into the fire, leaped on his horse and rode rapidly away. As I rejoined Ruth I wondered indeed if I were the double of some person who had died suddenly around here a few years ago.

When we resumed trailing again, Ruth took the lead, I the rear to push the reluctant O'Hara. Clouds sweeping the surface of this high plateau frequently engulfed us, so that even though only a hundred feet apart, we were invisible to each other as we called out of the grey swirling fog. Sometimes we could see only the legs and feet of our horses.

Suddenly Ruth called back.

"It looks as if we have come to the end of the earth. We're going to fall off!"

The descent was precipitous. We dropped into a dark forested canyon and the clouds crowded into the trees. A dozen sliding switchbacks down, we found the bottom and a stream chattering around buffalo-sized boulders.

Across the stream we commenced a long climb up the other side of the canyon. Fog swirled among the trees and pressed down on us, muffling the sounds of our passage. A little lake nestled at the foot of a rockslide, and, when the fog lifted momentarily, we saw ahead of us a row of fang-like peaks, several of them disappearing into the clouds.

"Do you think we will have to go through those?" Ruth asked.

"The horses will never make it," I answered.

The little lake was apparently the top of the climb for we again started to descend, dropping out of the clouds into a brush-filled swale that barred forward vision.

Then I heard a cry of delight from Ruth. She had emerged from the brush and was sitting, transfixed, gazing at the view in front of and below her.

A great valley, its floor more than a mile wide, swept from left to right in front of us and a mile below. On the far side, forming its

164

southern perimeter, a row of snow-covered mountains rose from the valley floor to tower above us, sustaining glaciers and festooned with waterfalls that gleamed and spread out like silvery veils. The valley floor, so flat that it looked like a lake surface covered with vegetation, drew our eyes westward, and we expected to see the sea. But there was only a sea of mountains rising to the sky. The valley, green with forest and interlaced with streams, had a road running down it connecting tiny clearings and toy buildings.

There, opposite us, rose Mackenzie's Stupendous Mountain and the rocky torch of Mount Nusatsum, the Mount Ararat of the local Indians, which, according to legend, offered a landing site from which the sole surviving canoe-load at the time of the world deluge descended to repopulate the earth.

"Look, look behind you!" Ruth exclaimed, and, turning in my saddle, I followed the direction of her pointing finger and saw a beetling precipice, sky-high and hanging out over the side of the valley. Softening the savage aspect, a thick necklace of white woolly cloud was strung like a garland across the lower part of the crag.

It was the Bella Coola Valley. We felt like victorious conquerors.

But it was 5,000 feet below, along many unknown miles of trail, so we bent to the task of moving our horses along the face of the mountain. Here indeed the caution advised by Paul Krestinuk was well-founded, for in some places the trail was only wide enough to allow a pack, and if there had been a stumble or a struggle for position between two horses, the loser would have tumbled not a thousand feet but three.

We reached timber, passed a lake and got into forests of pine, spruce and cedar, obtaining occasional glimpses of the valley floor, which seemed now to be coming up to meet us.

On a sandy ridge in the forest, three little grave-houses, a village of the dead, stood beside the trail, a gleaming white one with freshly moved earth indicating the burial we had been told about a few days ago.

Under these houses the Carriers now bury their dead. Not many decades ago they cremated the remains. We were shortly to learn that in the Bella Coola Valley, tree burials took place: the coffin was lashed in a high crotch in a big tree to stay there until the ropes rotted and the box and its contents came crashing to earth. Farther out, on the coast, where everything above high-tide mark was either rock or muskeg, interment took place in houses large enough to receive many dead, the boxes being stacked one on another, as goods in a warehouse.

Minutes after this we emerged onto the valley floor, where it was flat, and we found that after walking for so long down the steep slope, it was quite difficult to adapt to level terrain. A road wide enough for a car lay at our feet, and on it were tire tracks.

"There are no meadows down in the valley," the Indians had told us. "You'll have to get pasture with a settler."

Down the road a quarter of a mile a rural delivery mailbox stood on a post, and a road leading into a group of buildings indicated a farmstead.

"I'll go in and see if we can get some horse feed," I said, dismounting.

A tall man with grey hair answered my knock at the door.

Yes, we could pasture our horses in his field, he told me, obviously studying me as he replied. Yes, we could camp in the same field ... few men with rimless glasses and a scholarly accent came asking for horse feed and a place to camp. Yes, this was the Bella Coola Valley and the road does run right to the ocean ...

"And where do you come from, may I ask?"

"Right now we just came off the mountain, but originally we came from Calgary."

"From Calgary? With horses?"

"Yes."

"How long did it take you?"

"We left on June 17."

"You mean, you rode all the way from Calgary, with horses? How many people in your party?"

166

"Two, my wife and myself. She is out at the road with the horses."

"I've changed my mind," the man said. "You may pasture your horses in the field but I'll not let you camp there."

"I'm sorry," I said. "We'll move … "

"What I mean is, you and your wife will honour this house by being our guests. Please hurry and get your wife."

I hurried. I don't remember walking back to Ruth but I remember telling her we were to be guests in a Bella Coola Valley home.

"We're so ragged," she gasped.

"No matter. We can wrap blankets around us if we are not decent."

"Well, you've got two pairs of overalls on so the holes in one cover the holes in the other."

"And we've done it! In a few days on this road we'll be at the Pacific Ocean."

I dropped to the ground, kissed the earth and then with soil on my nose and lips, pulled Ruth down to where I could kiss her, too. Before we set out, she had made the same promise as her Biblical namesake, "Whither thou goest, I will go," and no one had ever fulfilled a promise in greater measure; nor had anyone contributed more to the success of an expedition than she.

Now, at this unusual salute, she spluttered and laughed; then, wiping the earth from our two faces, she followed as I led the way beneath towering cedar and fir trees.

Our host, Mr. John Hober and his wife, met us at their door. She drew Ruth into the house while Mr. Hober and I unpacked. The four packing boxes stacked in the shelter of the rose arbour seemed indeed a tiny bit of equipment with which to tackle three major mountain ranges and 1,500 miles of mountain trails. The horses, for the first time in four months, were turned loose without a bell. I was assured that the fences were good.

We stayed for two days.

Two hundred yards from the Hober home, a site marked by mounds of rotten timbers sinking into the ground and covered with moss showed the remains of the Indian village that had received, feted and feasted the explorer whose trail we had been following. Mackenzie wrote that he slept under "no other canopy than the sky; but I never enjoyed a more sound and refreshing rest, though I had a board for my bed and a billet for my pillow." Now we in our turn had a feast of roast chicken, fresh homemade bread warm from the oven, piles of fruit, bowls of whipped cream, and, that night, for the first time in four months, we slept under a roof more extensive than a ranger's cabin, slept indeed in a feather bed, and, like Mackenzie, "never enjoyed a more sound and refreshing rest."

Our plunge into the Bella Coola Valley was really an entry into an entirely new world much different from the Carrier country or that of the gold-seekers, and vastly different from the Alberta prairies. Here there was an abundance of food and shelter in the endless forest of huge trees and the salmon-filled streams that flowed through them. Here all a man needed to convert the trees of the forest into a snug log house was his two hands and a few simple tools. Mr. Hober showed how a froe splits shakes (lifetime shingles) out of a cedar block, how a chalk line snapped along a log marked guide lines for the great broad axes that craftsmen swung to produce mill-accurate and planer-smooth timbers.

Kahylsk Creek, now known as Burnt Bridge Creek, was the Indian name for the stream Mackenzie had followed into the valley.

"More correctly it is Burnt Bridges Creek. One bridge burned in a forest fire and a second one caught fire when two young fellows, after an evening of swapping bear stories, had to walk home in the dark. They were sure they heard a dozen bears in the woods and lit a fire in the biggest open space, the bridge, and burned it down."

The Hobers had come to this spot from Minnesota in 1906 with their four children. Their home became the district post office, called Sloan. But because there was another Sloane (with an "e") post office in British Columbia, the name was changed in 1912 to one Mr. Hober suggested: Firvale.

Mount Nusatsum, the "Mount Ararat" of the local Aboriginal peoples, rises over the Bella Coola Valley.

When Mackenzie left his host Indian village — which he called Friendly Village, for obvious reasons — he was taken down the river by seven of the tribesmen in two long cedar dugout canoes. He said in his diary, "I had imagined that the Canadians who accompanied me were the most expert canoemen in the world, but they were very inferior to these people, as they themselves acknowledged, in conducting these vessels."

The road we followed from friendly Firvale led many times through forests that met overtop, high overtop, and shut out the sky. Several groups of men were cutting and burning the huge fir and cedar trees to enlarge their clearings. At the foot of Mount Nusatsum, which rises to nearly 9,000 feet above the valley floor, we rode for two hours in its shade. We rode past orchards where abundant fruit hung on the trees, and between fields of potatoes, where crops had been harvested, the ground was freckled with potatoes left because they were too big or too small or had a bump on them.

Farther down the valley, the clearing merged and the homes were closer together. Then there was the fine white church, its steeple raised and its roof paralleling the lines of Mount Nusatsum, the Ararat of the Indians.

But the Indians called the mountain "Noosgultz" which meant "Mountain-With-A-Rope." With the new-fallen snow on the peak we could see the white band around the prominent prong that testified to the story that the cedar bark rope had been left tied there.

Toward evening we came to the establishment of storekeeper Carl Skjepstad where, Mr. Hober had told us, we would be able to get pasture for our horses. This little old frontier merchant kept store in a small log building situated among fruit trees. When we told him we had come from Calgary with packhorses, he sucked his cheeks in between his teeth and blinked his eyes rapidly and repeatedly in amazement.

Why, yes, we could camp in his orchard. Just turn the horses loose. People will keep the gate closed. And help yourself to the apples — all you want. Nah, nah. Money was not wanted. Get the water from the well, and there is dry wood in the shed.

When the tent was up, I went to the well for water. A square box with a lid on it and a pail hanging by a rope from a pole marked the site. The pole, with the pail at one end, was fastened on a big bolt driven into an upright post and had a rock fastened at the other end. When wanting water, which was within a few feet of the ground surface, one opened the hinged lid of the box, pulled down on the rope until the pail dipped into the water (tipping was assured by a weight fastened to one lip), then pulled it up, full, counterbalanced by the weight of the rock at the other end of the pole.

Next morning, five or six miles nearer the sea, we came to the home of the Hobers' daughter, Laura, who, with her husband Frank Ratcliff, invited us to camp and use their pasture as long as we liked.

It was seven miles to the wharf, "at the foot of the mountain you see down there, that big one coming in from the left. That next one is down channel about 20 miles … "

And so we set up camp, a comfortable one with a wide, deep bed of boughs and a pile of wood, and our possessions were all stacked within the tent.

That afternoon, October 10, we left Dream and O'Hara in the Ratcliff pasture and rode to the village of Bella Coola, which

Mackenzie had found an Aboriginal village on the Bella Coola River consisting of "six very large houses, erected on palisades, rising 25 feet from the ground … From these houses I could perceive the termination of the river and its discharge into a narrow arm of the sea."

consisted of some scattered houses almost hidden among the trees. The village had engineered streets, a school, stores, a church and a hospital, which was more civilization than we had seen in 300 miles.

Not a hundred yards from here, Mackenzie had found the Indian village on the Bella Coola River consisting of "six very large houses, erected on palisades, rising 25 feet from the ground ... From these houses I could perceive the termination of the river and its discharge into a narrow arm of the sea."

The explorer, possibly conditioned by the friendly reception he had received along the river, was surprised and dismayed by the lack of cordiality with which these people received him. A group of men "who returned from fishing had no more than five salmons; they refused to sell them, but gave me one roasted, of a very indifferent kind." His pique intensified next morning when he had difficulty getting a canoe to proceed down the channel; and when on his return several days later he had trouble with the Indians, his anger reached an all-time high and he called the place Rascal's Village.

This village had long disappeared, the site probably washed away by the Bella Coola River, and its people, or their descendants, had moved across the river beyond a strip of woods. A cable bridge for pedestrians only now swung across the river, giving access to the Indian village and affording a view of "the termination of the river."

We followed the road westward past the little village of the whites and in about half a mile, where the point of a promontory had been cut to accommodate the road, we came in view of the sea. Across several hundred yards of brown grass, another hundred of mud exposed by the low tide, it lay like a great grey lake, the head of North Bentinck Arm, the Pacific Ocean, our destination!

Yet our jubilation was tinged with disappointment. Reared far from the ocean, we had envisaged a shining silvery sea stretching to the west, with great breakers curling in to crash on the sandy beach. This day the clouds were lowering, hiding the mountaintops. Occasional foggy rain swept down. There was no wind and the mud

Two Aboriginal children on a street in the Bella Coola village about 1900.

of the tide flats in no way resembled a hard sandy beach. We had seen scores of mountain lakes much more impressive.

But it was indeed the ocean, the object of Mackenzie's quest and the Mecca towards which we had turned our faces every morning for the last 16 weeks.

I said to Ruth, "Bella Coola is where Alexander Mackenzie reached the sea, and where today we, Ruth and Cliff Kopas, have likewise reached the sea."

She nodded. "Let's congratulate ourselves," then laughing, she pointed to the gleaming mud at the edge of the tidal water. "Are you going to kiss the bottom of the ocean at Bella Coola too?"

We took our horses as far west as we could, to the end of the dock where the weekly steamer had the night before discharged a cargo of mail and "city supplies," and there we claimed the suitcases that had been forwarded by Ruth's sister to be here on our arrival.

That night, for the first time in four months, Ruth wore a dress and I exchanged rags for a suit. Footwear that had been on the point of surrendering to canvas wrappings was finally discarded in favour of city shoes.

That night, the tent illuminated by the flickering orange light of two candles (two rather than one by way of celebration) and warmed by the puffing little tin stove, we decided we would make our home in the Bella Coola Valley.

I wrote in my diary: "We reached the sea five days ahead of schedule. Fifteen hundred miles. The Bella Coola Valley is the most beautiful spot we have ever seen. It has never seen a depression. It has an air of contentment, like that of an old mountaineer smoking his carved pipe and watching the evening shadows rise out of the valley below. We will stay here."

And we did.

AFTERWORD

This beautiful valley did indeed become their home. Cliff wrote that during their first winter, a snug cabin under the mountains, loaned to them by Frank Ratcliff in return for doing a few chores, became the base for forays through the snows of winter, and that the orchard trees in spring blossomed in perfumed profusion.

Cliff described the valley as a meeting place of people of various ethnic origins and the Nuxalk of Bella Coola, who retained vestiges of their salmon-and-cedar civilization. Summer visits from the Aboriginal peoples of Anahim Lake and Ulkatcho brought a buckskin civilization to mingle with the existing cultures. Buildings were made of hand-hewn planks and many older folk spoke no English.

In early spring, Dr. H. A. MacLean planned a visit to a logging camp down the channel on the fish packer *J and J*, named for John and Johanna Harestad. There would be room aboard for Cliff and Ruth. Would they like to go? "We'll be going right by Mackenzie's Rock."

The final leg of the journey in the footsteps of Alexander Mackenzie was accomplished to the accompaniment of a throbbing, well-cared-for diesel engine. At Mackenzie's Rock, a white obelisk of cement marked where the explorer had spent the night. By contrast, Ruth and Cliff were guests at the Gildersleve Logging

After four months spent slogging through the wilderness, Ruth exchanges her trail clothes for a dress.

Company camp nearby, and neither starvation, Natives, nor anything else was a problem.

The second winter saw them comfortably settled in the caretaker's suite at the hospital. Dr. MacLean explained, "We like to have a man around the building at night in case of trouble, and the previous caretaker moved because there wasn't room for his family."

Ruth and Cliff's family was about to grow as well; the news of Ruth's pregnancy was welcomed, and plans for the home they wished to build "somewhere around" were discussed more earnestly. However, Ruth experienced serious complications as the pregnancy progressed, and shortly after giving birth to me, she died in February 1935, 16 months after their triumphant arrival in Bella Coola.

Crushed by the loss of his beloved companion, Cliff drew some comfort from his rich store of memories, and his recollection of Ruth's philosophy that never bowed to the finality of death. "We live on, in another form, maybe in another place," she had said.

Ruth was comforted in her final days by the presence of her sister, Violet Cole, who had been notified by wire of her illness and had come out from Calgary to help care for her. After Ruth's death, Violet and her husband, Peard, adopted me and lovingly raised me as their own in Calgary. When I was seven years old, Violet died; Peard later married Catherine Wylie, who became my third mother and the one who saw me through my formative years.

Cliff remained in Bella Coola, remarried and raised three sons and a daughter. He enjoyed a successful life as a father, businessman, writer, photographer and strong promoter of the Bella Coola Valley. Through the subsequent years, Cliff kept in contact with my adoptive parents and myself, and later, the strong personal bonds between Cliff and his second wife, Mae Edwards, and my own family — my wife Joanne, son Scott, and daughters Heather and Shelley — were strengthened through our mutual visits to Calgary and Bella Coola. To this day we remain in close touch with Cliff's daughter Rene and her husband John in Bella Coola. My father died in Bella Coola in 1978.

The Goat River Trail, one of the more arduous trails described in *Packhorses to the Pacific*, was established in 1886 to link the historic gold-mining town of Barkerville with the Fraser River to the east. The trail was heavily used in the early 1900s but was virtually unidentifiable when Cliff and Ruth made their journey in 1933. It remained in a state of disrepair until the 1990s, when the Fraser River Alliance undertook a restoration program. To this day, the Goat River Trail portion, from McBride to Bowron Lake (described in Cliff's book as "a highway of high hopes and deep despair"), can only be traversed on foot, although, thanks to the dedicated efforts of the Alliance, it has been much improved.

In August 2000 the trail was officially dedicated as part of the National Hiking Trail. It was a great honour for Rene and me to

A large boulder still bears Mackenzie's triumphant proclamation: Alex Mackenzie from Canada by land 22 July 1793.

be part of the ceremony and to be standing in "Kopas Camp," the first campsite west of Crescent Spur on the Fraser River at the east end of the trail. Today, the 95-kilometre trail can be hiked in five to seven days, beginning at Crescent Spur on Highway 16 north of McBride and culminating at Bowron Lake Provincial Park.

The original edition of *Packhorses to the Pacific* was given to me with this accompanying letter:

> Dear Keith,
>
> The enclosed copy of the book tells the story to the public of the packhorse trip to the Pacific. What I could not express, because it was far too personal, was the intense love and respect which I held for your mother and which now attends her memory. I hope the book meets with your approval.

It is with pride that we once again provide this story of love and adventure to you. We hope the pictures of the Goat River Trail have added an enjoyable dimension.

Keith Cole

Keith Cole and sister Rene Morton proudly stand in front of the trailhead sign marking the Goat River section of the National Hiking Trail.

This placid view of the Goat River belies the trail's long history as "a highway of high hopes and deep despair."

179

INDEX

ABOUT THE AUTHOR

Cliff Kopas was born and raised in southern Alberta from where, as a teenager, he undertook packhorse trips into the nearby Rocky Mountains. In 1933, he and his first wife Ruth settled in Bella Coola, where Cliff worked as a writer and photographer while supplementing his income as a fish guardian and bookkeeper.

In 1937, together with his second wife Mae, he opened a general store, which continues in business to this day. Cliff and Mae were active in the community and prominent in the completion of the "Freedom Road" portion of the famous Chilcotin Highway. In addition to *Packhorses to the Pacific* (1976), he wrote *Bella Coola* (1970) and *No Path But My Own* (completed by his son Leslie in 1996.)

Back cover photos (counter-clockwise from top right): Graveyard Flats, Alberta, by Gillean Daffern; Elbow Lake, Alberta, by Gillean Daffern; east entrance of Tweedsmuir Park by Al Nickull; Barkerville by Jayne Seagrave; "Kopas Camp," part of the National Hiking Trail, by Keith Cole.

Inside photos: pages 22, 118, 120, 122, Heritage House Collection; page 173 by I. Fougner; page 179 by Keith Cole; all other photos by Cliff and Ruth Kopas, courtesy of Keith Cole.